THE HUGO BOSS PRIZE 2002

THE HUGO BOSS PRIZE 2002

Guggenheim Museum

Francis Alÿs
Olafur Eliasson
Hachiya Kazuhiko
Pierre Huyghe
Koo Jeong-a
Anri Sala

Published following the selection of the
finalists for The Hugo Boss Prize 2002.

The Hugo Boss Prize 2002 © 2002 The
Solomon R. Guggenheim Foundation,
New York. All rights reserved.

ISBN 3-7757-1233-X

Guggenheim Museum Publications
1071 Fifth Avenue
New York, New York 10128

Distributed in Europe by
Hatje Cantz Verlag
Senefelderstrasse 12
73760 Ostfildern/Ruit, Germany

Design:
COMA Amsterdam/New York
coma@aya.yale.edu
Production:
Tracy L. Hennige, Beth Levy,
Melissa Secondino
Editorial:
Meghan Dailey, Elizabeth Franzen,
Carey Ann Schaefer, Edward Weisberger,
Jennifer Knox White
Translation:
Connie Prener/Eriksen Translations

Printed in The Netherlands
by Veenman drukkers, Ede

Contents

Marjetica Potrč, *Kagiso: Skeleton House*, 2000–01.
Two structures made from concrete blocks, bricks, wood, corrugated fiberglass paneling, corrugated metal sheathing, saturated roofing felt, and other building materials; skeleton house: 8 feet 11 inches x 23 feet 7 inches x 17 feet 7 inches (271.8 x 718.8 x 535.9 cm); shack: 7 feet 11 inches x 15 feet 10 inches x 9 feet 4 inches (241.3 x 482.6 x 114.5 cm). Solomon R. Guggenheim Museum, New York. Purchased with funds contributed by the Young Collectors Council, 2001.27.

Preface
Dr. Bruno Sälzer

We are delighted to celebrate the presentation of The Hugo Boss Prize for the fourth time. This award is the result of many years of fruitful cooperation between Hugo Boss and the Solomon R. Guggenheim Museum. Together we have succeeded in establishing a forum for recognizing outstanding achievements in contemporary art—an accomplishment in which we take great satisfaction and that articulates our continued dedication to the arts.

The nominated artists hail from many different countries and represent a diverse range of genres, including short films and videos, video installations, performance, photography, and sculpture. This is art that invites the viewer to transcend borders and definitions, to experience inspiration, provocation, and sometimes alienation. Tolerance and open-mindedness are essential. Ostensible opposites are reconciled. Minds are opened. For us, embracing differences and new perspectives constitutes the foremost challenge posed by contemporary art, and it is our goal to promote this spirit of innovation and diversity.

We would like to express our sincere thanks to the members of the international jury for their excellent and thought-provoking selections. We are also, of course, most indebted to the short-listed artists, as well as to Susan Cross, Assistant Curator, for her organization of the 2002 Hugo Boss Prize, and to Nancy Spector, Curator of Contemporary Art, for her continued support of this project. Finally, a very special note of thanks goes to Thomas Krens, Director, for his ongoing commitment to the award.

Dr. Bruno Sälzer
Chairperson and CEO
HUGO BOSS AG

Douglas Gordon, *through a looking glass*, 1999.
Color video and audio installation with two projections, dimensions variable. Edition 3/3. Solomon R. Guggenheim Museum, New York, Purchased with funds contributed by the International Director's Council and Executive Committee Members: Edythe Broad, Henry Buhl, Elaine Terner Cooper, Gail May Engelberg, Linda Fischbach, Ronnie Heyman, Dakis Joannou, Cindy Johnson, Barbara Lane, Linda Macklowe, Peter Norton, Willem Peppler, Denise Rich, Simonetta Seragnoli, David Teiger, Ginny Williams, Elliot Wolk, 1999.5304.

Acknowledgments

Thomas Krens

Two thousand and two marks the fourth time the Guggenheim will award the Hugo Boss Prize to a contemporary artist who is profoundly affecting current trends. In so doing, we hope to promote the spirit of exploration and ingenuity so critical to the museum's mission and to the vitality of the visual arts. An integral component of the Guggenheim's contemporary art programming since its inception in 1996, the biannual prize—which includes a generous grant of $50,000—has given us the opportunity to acknowledge and support the work of extraordinary talents who are actively redefining the parameters of today's cultural production. By casting a wide net—the prize sets no restrictions in terms of age, gender, race, nationality, or chosen artistic medium—we have succeeded in creating a forum for international artists using diverse modes of expression. The distinctive work and backgrounds of the recipients of the first three prizes—Matthew Barney, Douglas Gordon, and Marjetica Potrč, who come from the United States, Scotland, and Slovenia respectively—attest to the global aspirations of the prize as well as its recognition of a range of aesthetic and conceptual approaches. The exceptional finalists for 2002—Francis Alÿs (born in Belgium, based in Mexico), Olafur Eliasson (Denmark; Germany), Hachiya Kazuhiko (Japan), Pierre Huyghe (France), Koo Jeong-a (Korea; Paris), and Anri Sala (Albania; France)—also represent the wide-reaching scope of the prize.

Beyond identifying and rewarding artists whose work both represents and influences significant developments in contemporary art, our goal is to introduce the work of these artists to a broader audience. Moreover, the museum maintains a continuing interest in the development of their careers. We are very pleased to have fostered relationships with previous finalists by acquiring and exhibiting their works.

Recently, the museum acquired Marjetica Potrč's architectural installation Kagiso: Skeleton House (2000–01), which was first presented at the exhibition honoring her as the recipient of the 2000 prize. In 1999, the museum was pleased to purchase through a looking glass, a significant video work by 1998 prize winner Douglas Gordon. This year, we are presenting a major exhibition of the work of Matthew Barney, opening in New York in February 2003 following a European debut. Organized for the museum by Nancy Spector, this exhibition features Barney's five-part Cremaster film cycle, including Cremaster 3, the final installment, which was filmed in part in the Guggenheim's Frank Lloyd Wright–designed rotunda. We look forward to continuing such rewarding exchanges with the artists we have come to know through the Hugo Boss Prize, past and present.

The first two Hugo Boss Prizes were complemented by an exhibition of the finalists' work installed at the Guggenheim Museum SoHo in advance of the announcement of the award. For the Hugo Boss Prize 2000, the work of the winning artist was presented in a special exhibition at the Guggenheim Museum uptown. In lieu of presenting the work of all the finalists, a magazine-like publication was designed as a portable exhibition of sorts. We continue this tradition again here, and each artist has been invited to contribute to the catalogue six pages of their own design, which articulate their aesthetic projects in two dimensions.

The organization of the Hugo Boss Prize is the result of collaborations between institutions and individuals to whom we are deeply indebted. Foremost, we are grateful for the unwavering commitment of Werner Baldessarini, former Chairman of the Management Board, Hugo Boss AG, and Dr. Bruno Sälzer, Chairperson and CEO, Hugo Boss AG. Hugo Boss's sponsorship of this award is but one example of the innovative cultural patronage that inspired this unique prize. We would also like to thank Dr. Hjoerdis Jahnecke, manager of art sponsorship at Hugo Boss, whose enthusiastic cooperation with the Guggenheim's staff in insuring the successful realization of this project epitomizes the friendship between our two organizations. Markus Aller, Online Editor, must also be recognized for his oversight of the informative and expansive Hugo Boss Prize Web site.

Perhaps the most difficult task in bringing this prize to fruition is that performed by the panel of jurors, who determine the finalists and, ultimately, the recipient of the prize. We were most fortunate to have been able to rely on the expertise, dedication, and good nature of my fellow jurors Sandra Antelo-Suarez, independent curator and Founder and Editorial Director, *Trans>arts.cultures.media*; Lisa Dennison, Deputy Director and Chief Curator, Guggenheim Museum; Yuko Hasegawa, Chief Curator, Twenty-first Century Museum of Contemporary Art, Kanazawa, Japan; Suzanne Pagé, Director, Musée d'Art Moderne de la Ville de Paris; and Nancy Spector, Curator of Contemporary Art, Guggenheim Museum. I appreciate their thoughtful deliberations during the selection process.

At the Guggenheim, we would like to thank Susan Cross, Assistant Curator, for her dedicated organization of all aspects of this project and the curatorial staff who have contributed to its realization: Lisa Dennison, Nancy Spector, and Assistant Curator Joan Young for their generous advice, and for their collegial support, we thank Tracey Bashkoff, Vivien Greene, Lisa Panzera, Fiona Ragheb, and Karole Vail. We would also like to express our appreciation to Kendall Hubert, Director of Corporate Development, for her essential role as liaison between the museum and Hugo Boss every step of the way. Our appreciation also goes to Betsy Ennis, Senior Publicist, and Sasha Nicholas, Public Affairs Coordinator, as well as Michael Lavin, Technical Director, and the Theater and Media Services staff for their contributions.

This publication is the result of the labors of many talented individuals. We would like to express our gratitude to authors Francesco Bonami, Yuko Hasegawa, Jörg Heiser, Nico Israel, James Rondeau, and Maria-Christina Villaseñor, whose essays provide valuable insights on the work of the finalists. Cornelia Blatter and Marcel Hermans of COMA are responsible for the catalogue's inventive and exciting design. Interns Debbie Pora Ahn, Marie von Fink, and especially Marta Ruperez provided invaluable research assistance and compiled the artists' exhibition histories. We are also indebted to those who have produced this catalogue: Elizabeth Levy, Managing Editor/Manager of Foreign Editions; Tracy L. Hennige, Production Assistant; Melissa Secondino, Associate Production Manager; Elizabeth Franzen, Manager of Editorial Services; editors Meghan Dailey, Carey Ann Schaefer, Edward Weisberger, and Jennifer Knox White; Administrative Assistant Stephen Hoban; and Connie Prener for her translation services. We also thank Ellen Labenski, Assistant Photographer, who was generous as always with her time and skill, and Kim Bush, Manager of Photography.

We are especially appreciative of the representatives of the artists, their assistants, and a host of individuals for their help throughout the preparatory stages of this project and the accompanying publication: Tanya Bonakdar Gallery, New York, particularly Ethan Sklar; Galerie Chantal Crousel, Paris, especially Niklas Svennung; Marian Goodman Gallery, Paris and New York, especially Catherine Belloy, Lissa McClure, and Anja Schneider; Galerie Yvon Lambert Paris and Olivier Belot; Lisson Gallery, London; Kaori Kamisawa, art cocoon, Tokyo; Caroline Eggel, Olafur Eliasson Studio; Zach Miner, Gagosian Gallery, New York; Patricia Brunerie, Musée d'Art Moderne de la Ville de Paris; Ritsu Yoshino, Twenty-first Century Museum of Contemporary Art, Kanazawa.

And finally, we offer our gratitude to the artists for the outstanding contributions they have made to the contemporary visual arts and to this catalogue.

Thomas Krens
Director
The Solomon R. Guggenheim Foundation

14

Matthew Barney, *CREMASTER 3*, 2002.
Production photograph.

Introduction

Susan Cross

The Rules of the Game

1. The artist must be making significant contributions to the contemporary visual arts.

2. The artist may be of any age, race, or nationality and may work in any medium.

Given the wealth of talented and innovative artists who can play by the above rules, it is no small feat that a Hugo Boss Prize shortlist of six or seven artists can be agreed upon. Having witnessed the challenging selection process, shaped by the diverse experience of the jurors and the relatively open-ended criteria for the prize, I have a keen appreciation for its inherent difficulty. Indeed, there is no doubt that many worthy artists are not included on our all-too-aptly termed short and, by its very nature, subjective list. But it is equally doubtless that the outstanding finalists for the 2002 prize—Francis Alÿs, Olafur Eliasson, Hachiya Kazuhiko, Pierre Huyghe, Koo Jeong-a, and Anri Sala—are profoundly influencing and expanding the visual arts.

Though selected for their individual accomplishments, these six artists, when considered collectively, help us identify current aesthetic and conceptual leanings. Despite the gravity of much of the content of their production, the 2002 finalists share a strong narrative impulse as well as a sense of play and an interest in games. In thinking about these strategies, I am reminded of Clue, the board game in which players must navigate a series of rooms and passages to reconstruct the elements of a murder mystery after the fact, with the evidence at hand: six possible suspects, six weapons, six different rooms. The object of the game—deducing a story by examining multiple clues—seems an apt metaphor for this year's finalists. Their work investigates the "playing field," as it were: the spaces where we interact and are acted upon, ranging from the city street to the museum to more metaphorical terrain, such as the political arena or the space of collective memory. In considering a variety of shared social spaces, the artists often emphasize collaboration with other artists, other disciplines, and the public, underscoring art's actual and potential role in the larger community and as a point of exchange.

They often do this with surprisingly subtle means. Koo Jeong-a's installations—made from materials as quiet and unassuming as mounds of crushed aspirin, arrangements or disarrangements of crumpled papers and piles of coins on a desk, or a simple change in the light source of a room—invite us to take on the role of detective and observe what we might usually fail to notice. In this way, a work like *Snowy Sunny Day* (1997) is reminiscent of a crime scene or, more innocently, the parlor game in which one thing is removed from a room, and everyone must then identify the missing object. Like that pastime, in which the moved article is often remembered by its relationship to another, Koo Jeong-a's work heightens our awareness of our environment and the connections between its markers, however small. Much as we connect particular moments in our histories to form memories, and thus our identity, the narrative in her work lies in the relationships between the viewer and disparate objects and territories. As Jean-Christophe Bailly has described it, Koo Jeong-a's work is "a pure relation of spaces and intervals," both "like a novel" and "a puzzle."[1] Divining these miniature cosmos—figuring out their system—and pondering the invisible hand and mind that constructed them, parallels larger musings about gods, myths of creation, and the origin of the universe: the ultimate "who dunnit."

Francis Alÿs is more overtly interested in narrative, equating his works with stories or modern fables that help make sense of place and experience. Through his walks in Mexico City and elsewhere, Alÿs creates and charts the activity of the streets. These walks, during which he subtly intervenes within the cityscape, are the seeds of urban myths. He maintains that his works are as simple as a joke that can be passed on and retold, like the one about the man who marked his path with the unraveled yarn of his sweater (*Untitled*, 1998). This walk through Stockholm—connecting two museums, one of modernist design, the other from the nineteenth century, symbolically bridging past and present—also conjures the story of Penelope and her undoing of Ulysses's shroud, or Hansel and Gretel leaving their trail of bread crumbs. As the best stories always are, this one is already somewhat familiar. While the origins of such fairy tales and parables may be forgotten, their core themes, morals, and structures remain, ready for individual or regional interpretations and flourishes. Likewise the postcards that Alÿs distributes in conjunction with his walks give instructions so that anyone might re-create his steps and put his stories in motion. As in the rules for a game, they are simple and allow anyone to play again and again.

Alÿs's ultimately collaborative intentions challenge traditional notions of the authority of the artist. His own tendency to "disappear" from his work is especially evident in *The Ambassador*, his contribution to the 2001 Venice *Biennale*, for which he dispatched a live peacock to act as his representative, as well as through his long-term collaboration with professional sign painters in Mexico. Their reinterpretations of Alÿs's drawings and paintings, coupled with the artist's own remaking of his works, parallel the transformations a story, and (hi)story, can take in the course of its telling and retelling.

Hachiya Kazuhiko's interactive art compels viewers to become active participants through gaming models. Works that incorporate swings, skateboard ramps, and sumo wrestling rings investigate how both children and adults can find answers about their lived experience by "acting out" scenarios within a prescribed arena. Hachiya's *Over the Rainbow* (1994) is a swing set that produces a rainbow spectrum of lights that illuminate the structure only when all the participants are swinging at different heights. This unexpected reward produced by accidental cooperation addresses both the potential and difficulty of successful communal efforts. At the core of Hachiya's utopian vision is heightened communication and empathy, which he combines in *PostPet* (1996–2002), a narrative software program for e-mail. *PostPet* makes technology appealing and offers a friendly way to grasp the workings of the Internet by creating digital creatures that live in fantastic homes on your computer desktop and deliver your e-mail. By introducing Post-

Pets—characters able to produce their own adventures with mislaid mail, undelivered or unexpected messages, and interactions with other PostPets—Hachiya makes a previously banal medium more interactive through storytelling and invites users to delight in what are usually frustrations, such as slow connections or maddening glitches that crash a computer. Technology is often decried as a dehumanizing force, yet in Hachiya's hands, individuality and intimacy are restored to anonymous, everyday exchanges through mechanized means.

Pierre Huyghe also explores the intersection of real and imaginary characters. His examination of narrative structures has focused on those of the cinema and the technological and personal aspects of filmmaking and viewing. Works such as *Remake* (1995), *Sleeptalking* (1998), and *The Third Memory* (1999) variously combine contemporary reenactments with interviews and original footage of Alfred Hitchcock's *Rear Window* (1954), Andy Warhol's *Sleep* (1963), and Sydney Lumet's *Dog Day Afternoon* (1975) respectively. The focus of Huyghe's works is on the actors themselves, whose interpretations of and deep engagement with the characters and stories are, for the artist, the more interesting drama. Like Clue, in which much of the action takes place "between" the rooms, or "scenes" of the crime, Huyghe is fascinated by the behind-the-scenes and interstitial spaces; he realizes that the game takes place as much in how the narrative is created as in the primary narrative itself.

Huyghe's interest in the role of "players" was explored again in *Atari Light* (1999), a room-size computer game mounted on the ceiling. Based on Pong, the first Atari video game, the work allows viewers to interact with it, but, as in a real game of Pong, participants are limited by Huyghe's preprogrammed conditions. In the French Pavilion at the 2001 Venice *Biennale*, this game room was situated between two other rooms containing installations by Huyghe; in order to move from one space to another, visitors had to go through separate entrances. As in a game, the rules governing Huyghe's installation choreograph our movements and echo the more invisible strictures we maneuver in our daily lives.

Anri Sala also manipulates various filmic conventions in his videos. Combining a wide range of techniques and styles, from film noir to documentary, he confuses the viewer's visual clues and concentrates on the intersection between fiction and reality, memory and truth. In *Intervista—quelques mots pour le dire* (Interview—finding the right words, 1997), Sala enacts his own detective story as he tries to recover a certain moment in his mother's history and that of his native Albania. The personal account he constructs within a larger historical narrative parallels our tendency to remember, digest, and mark historical events by our own experiences of them. Likewise, in *Byrek* (2000), the artist addresses the loss of tradition and the rupture in Eastern European culture through a narrative about his separation from his grandmother. As Sala grapples with his own experience through stories, so too do the others he records in his works. In *Nocturnes* (1999), two residents of Tourcoing, France, recount their histories and attempt to make sense of their situations through more manageable narratives, which nonetheless mirror their own; the lonely outsider finds a community in his tanks of exotic fish, and the confused ex-soldier processes his past aggressions by playing video games. Focusing more specifically on play, *Missing Landscape* (2001) shows repeating scenes of a boys' soccer game. The subtle, cyclical action suggests a larger metaphor of recurrence: despite the lessons learned or the stories told before, history will continue to repeat itself.

With his simulations of natural phenomenon, Olafur Eliasson challenges the many myths that govern our accepted realities. In *The double sunset* (1999), for which the artist manufactured a glowing second sun with visible metal scaffolding and spotlights, Eliasson contradicts the metanarrative—one side framed as the mysterious realm of the spiritual, the other as the debased product of man—that divides nature from culture. In this work and others, Eliasson does not hide the mechanisms he uses to create his perceptual play. Exposing the methods of fabrication and freeing us from the romantic notions of nature as a superior force, he allows us to take as much pleasure in his man-made phenomena as we do in their "natural" counterparts. In *The mediated motion* (2001), a recent installation for the Kunsthaus Bregenz, Eliasson planted duckweed in a pond he had constructed inside the museum's concrete building. Appearing unexpectedly at home in its indoor environment, this living, growing piece was made all the more surprising by another intervention. Subverting the usual customs that guide and regulate our movement—and often without our awareness—museum visitors had to traverse pathways that allowed only one way in and out of the galleries, the only other choice being an obvious dead end, like that in a maze. Urging us to rely on instinct, Eliasson heightens our awareness of ourselves and our surroundings. He asks us to be our own barometer, to measure conditions subjectively, despite assumptions mandating an understanding of nature through science. In other words, he stages the viewer as the protagonist of the experience, as evidenced in *The drop factory: a short story on your self ref and rep* (2000). Like many of his works, this piece turns a mirror, both literally and metaphorically, onto the viewer.

Mapping out connections between these six diverse artists, like stars in a constellation, is a means to situate them within the greater cultural landscape. Their shared examination and use of games and narrative allow us (and them) to assume other guises, live out fears and fantasies, and experience both victory, loss and pleasure and pain, at a safe remove. It is this projection, ordering, and mediation of our experience that these six artists variously mimic, manipulate, and deconstruct.

1   Jean-Christophe Bailly, "Latest News from the Expanse," in *Koo Jeong-a*, exh. cat. (Paris: Yvon Lambert, 2001), pp. 126–28.

oo Jeong-a, *Untitled*, 2001. C-print, 58 1/4 x 39 1/3 inches.

Francis Alÿs, *The Ambassador*, Venice, 2001.

Hachiya Kazuhiko, *PostPet*, 1996–2002. Computer (mailing) software. Original plan and direction by the artist; graphic design: Manabe Namie; programming and engineering: Koki Takashi.

Pierre Huyghe, *Atari Light*, 1999. Computer game program, interface, joysticks, and mixed media. Edition of 2, 1 A.P. Installation for the 49th Venice *Biennale*, 2001.

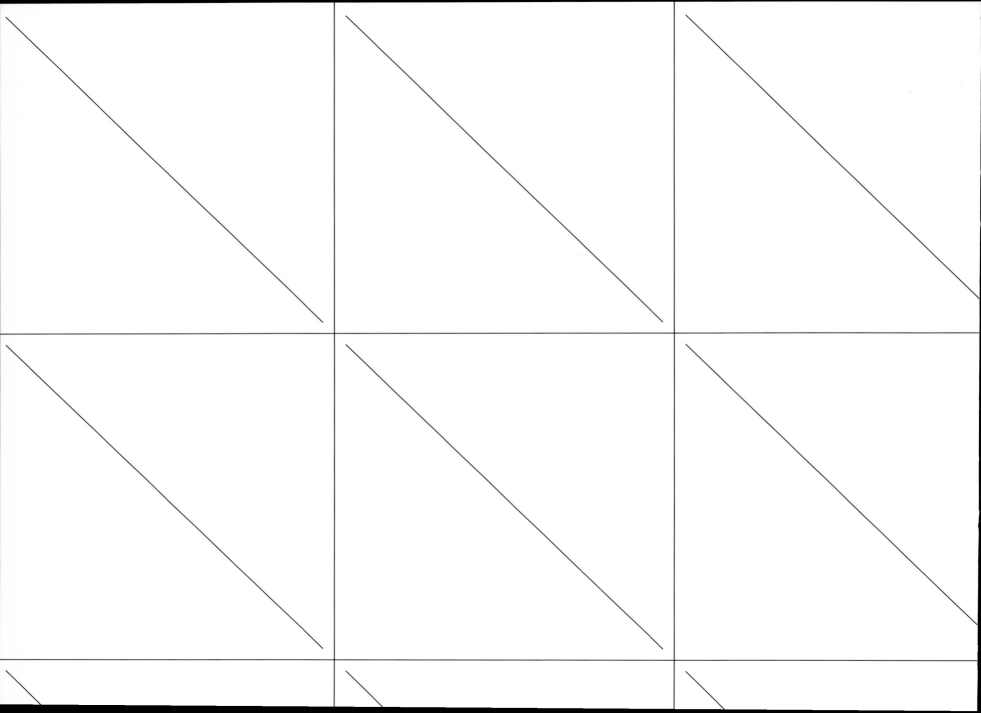

Footnotes: On Francis Alÿs

Nico Israel

In the "Proteus" chapter of James Joyce's *Ulysses*, a saturnine Stephen Dedalus is taking a walk along the seaside south of Dublin. He is alone; it is a June day. He is wearing hand-me-down boots that do not fit. He muses about the midwife who dragged him into the world, telephones, Paris, his dead mother, popular songs, and Yeatsian poems. The rhythmic sounds of his steps on sand and seashells lead him to ruminate about the way history works. Does it march forward toward a goal, or is it recursive and meandering? Does it ever stand still? Stephen encounters the carcass of a dead dog, lying in the ocean, being sniffed at by another, living dog, Tatters. Stephen thinks of dogs and God, scribbles a little note, hides it in a rock, then pees in the ocean.

I begin with a brief invocation of this notoriously arcane text as a way of making an initial approach to Francis Alÿs's art, not only because "Proteus" is the most poignant rendering of walking and thinking I know, but also because—as different as Joyce's modernism is from Alÿs's art—many of the motifs generated in the chapter connect integrally with aspects of the artist's practice. There is, foremost, the act of walking, which forms the core of Alÿs's project, even when that act is not directly depicted as or in an image. There are boots—feet and their coverings being a necessary focal point in Alÿs's walks—and dogs, which appear frequently as figures for tenacity, suffering, and, occasionally, strutting exuberance. And rather more abstractly, there is the question of the narrativity of history (and art history) that Alÿs's protean artwork addresses as a hidden note to an unknown, unseen viewer. Following in the footsteps of Joyce and Alÿs, then, I propose incursions into these four fundamental concepts of Alÿs's art: walking, shoes, dogs, (hi)stories. If the path seems to meander, the narrative stray off course—or, say, into a footnote—that is very much in the digressive, parapatetic spirit of the art.

The first time I saw one of Alÿs's works was in 1998 at the São Paolo *Bienal*. A video portrayed a lanky European—Alÿs himself—pushing a large block of ice through the streets of Mexico City. The camera followed him for nine hours as he performed his pseudo-Sisyphean task, recording the neighborhoods of the city as though incidentally, until the ice, initially a perfect Minimalist cube, became a kickable fragment and then, finally, a little puddle of water. A companion video traced the progress of a plastic bottle as it was pushed around the streets near the Zócalo, the city's main square, narrowly avoiding being trampled by passersby and cars. The two-video installation was called *Paradox of Praxis* (1997), the paradox contained in the two parenthetical subtexts "Sometimes making something leads to nothing" (ice block) and "Sometimes making nothing leads to something" (bottle). But the video depictions of these two types of "walking" clearly demonstrated that something *always* happens: In his art, the something/happening is public, site (or city) specific, and ineluctably visible, if often only peripherally so.

This is true of Alÿs's other streetwalking projects: In *Magnetic Shoes* (1994), he walked through the neighborhoods of Havana with footwear made of magnets; in *Leak* (1995), first enacted for a gallery in Ghent, he carried an open, dripping can of paint so that it looped from gallery to city center, before leading him back, breadcrumb-like, to the gallery;[1] for *Narcotourism* (1996), he took a different illicit drug each day for a week—hashish, ecstasy, heroin, and others—and sauntered into Copenhagen's city center. In each of these walks—with their subsequent multiple (re-) renderings in the form of postcards, photographs, drawings, and paintings (made by Alÿs himself and hired Mexican professional street painters, or *rotulistas*)[2]—what seems most salient is that walking is somehow exteriorized, turned from a figure of melancholic self-absorption (as with Joyce's Stephen Dedalus) into a specific public *inscription*.

Many have noted parallels between Alÿs's pedestrian peregrinations and Baudelaire's conception of *flânerie*, but a comparison reveals how significantly presumptions about art, the artist, and "modern life" have changed.[3] Alÿs is not merely an anonymous spectator tapping into what he calls the crowd's "electrical energy"; his walks are public and visible, and they often interrupt the flows of the city. While Baudelaire's painter is supposed to be "at home" everywhere, Alÿs's work reveals that he feels and acts like a tourist everywhere, even when "at home."[4] Alÿs disturbs Baudelaire's very idea of the artist located at the "center of the world" by frequently focusing on so-called peripheral places—Mexico City, Havana, Lima—cities with sometimes disastrous relations to modernity and globalization. Perhaps most important, unlike Baudelaire's artist, Alÿs says he has no ambition for his art to be "more living than life itself" and stand the test of time; for him, an art of the never-ending "now" would suffice.

In *Paradox of Praxis*, the walker wears green Converse All Star high-tops; in *Leak*, the sneakers are white. In some works from the series *The Liar, The Copy of the Liar* (1994), a generic executive is shown in a business suit and brown leather lace-ups. In *Magnetic Shoes*, plimsouls made of magnets attract ephemera from the Cuban soil. In documents of these walk-works, Alÿs minimizes his bodily presence; we rarely see his head or face and do not hear his voice. Instead, shoes are the viewer's entryway into the work. At issue in Alÿs's choice of footwear, then, is not comfort or fashion. Instead, it can become a social sign, generating a multiplicity of possible narratives—the All Stars perhaps signifying the international slacker artist/intellectual; the leather lace-ups, invoking the ad-propagated vision of a young businessman; the Havana shoes, pulling the city into their force field.

There is, of course, a long-running debate over the representation of shoes in art, from Heidegger-Schapiro-Derrida's extended excursus on their meaning in Vincent van Gogh's paintings to Fredric Jameson's interpretation of Andy Warhol's series *Diamond Dust Shoes* (1980) as signs of a nascent postmodernism. Alÿs's focus on footwear serves as a kind of downward displacement of these metaphysical questions into the material realm of walking. The very dynamism of his steps reveals all attempts to freeze the shoes into a kind of icon for art or the artist are theoretical faux pas: Art, his projects seem to suggest, does not come "poetically" from the earth (as Martin Heidegger claims) but is linked to the politics of site specificity; it is not restricted to biography or historical context (Meyer Schapiro's concerns), but calls those very concepts into question. If art deals with "truth" (the question Jacques Derrida asks), it does so in a decidedly circuitous way (hence, the implicit warning of Alÿs's title *The Liar*) and, contrary to the "waning of affect" linked by Jameson to a U.S.–dominated form of globalization, Alÿs's work, which is anything but unfeeling, snide, or dryly Conceptualist, shows us that globalization does not have to equal economic or cultural homogenization.

In American slang, feet are sometimes called "dogs," and in Alÿs' work there does seem to be an intimate connection between human feet and dogs' bodies. For one of his earliest projects, *The Collector* (1991–92), Alÿs walked around Mexico City, Alfred Jarry–style, with a rectangular magnet on wheels, about the size of a bichon frisé, attached to a leash. This canine—which Alÿs explains was designed as a prototype for a large edition of urban toys—recalls the Havana magnetic shoes in its intervention in the cityscape as a conversation piece and curiosity, while simultaneously culling something from the city. Although this dog is inanimate, there are also an impressive number of live canines pictured in his work—in part simply because stray dogs are so prevalent on the streets of Mexico City—but the presence of dogs also has explicit sociopolitical overtones as well. *The Story of Negrito* (1997), which the artist printed on bright posters, concerns precisely such a stray dog. "Once upon a time," the story begins, "there lived a dog called Negrito," who, "like all the mutts who run around the city," spent his day sniffing, scrounging, and snoozing—until he was run over by a police patrol car and left for dead. Yet the brave and plucky Negrito, who lost a leg, survived, and learned to walk again. And, as the poster informs us with morbid concision, "he was resolved to turn bad luck to advantage": Negrito learned how to juggle the bone of his own severed leg for captivated audiences.

In photographs from the *Sleepers* series (1999; 2001), Alÿs documents various mongrels curled up on sidewalks or under bridges, while in neighboring images, we see homeless or destitute men in similar positions. By invoking the comparison, he raises questions about the representability of suffering in art with a striking visual economy and sympathy. He also deftly directs our attention to the intimate relation between suffering and political power; after all, it is no accident that Negrito was run over by a police car.[5]

In Alÿs's latest work (in preparation as this essay goes to press), he proposes to hang a painting—depicting a multi-ethnic riot reminiscent of Paolo Uccello's *Battle of San Romano* (ca. 1430)—in a museum in Los Angeles. "As the museum opens its doors to the public," Alÿs's directions read, "a carrier" removes the painting from the wall and "takes it for a walk through the city." As night and closing time approaches, "the carrier brings the painting back to the museum, hangs it on the wall, and covers it with a veil" so it can "sleep." Few will see this work in the museum; it will be activated as it is placed in (loco)motion, and taken through various neighborhoods. As the painting circulates, it will remind Los Angeles residents of their most painful recent historical episode—the widely televised 1992 riots—thus reopening a social wound that public officials have sought to close off and render an aberration of the distant past.

This work seems emblematic of Alÿs's conception of his-

tory, which depends on our ability to tell ourselves stories—the kind of circuitous, tattered, unending stories we tell ourselves when we walk. His art never ignores history's wounds—indeed it could be said constantly to be scratching, mutt-like, at those very wounds—but it also intimately engages the question of how individual thoughts, narratives, and memories intersect with others in the matrix of social, communal space, producing new narratives that, with their own levity, can counteract the gravity of history. If official, date-driven history exists like monuments exist in the cityscape, then public, everyday history is no more vertical and unidirectional than is a stroll on the beach or a bottle being blown by the wind. Alÿs's art alerts us to the fact that, as with a shaggy dog story, we never know where the next step might lead, except, perhaps, on to the next step.[6]

All quotes from the artist are from correspondence with the author unless otherwise noted.

1. Alÿs evocatively describes his ambivalent relationship to institutional spaces: "No matter how much I intend to function outside the white cube, my identity as an artist irresistibly pulls me back, as if a long elastic was attached."
2. Alÿs collaborated with Mexican sign painters for four years. He says that he was "trying to propose an alternative to the commercial system," both of advertising and of the art market. The aim was also to "confuse concepts of authorship and originality through unlimited editions."
3. "For the perfect flâneur. . . it is an immense joy to set up house in the heart of the multitude, amid the ebb and flow of movement, in the midst of the fugitive and the infinite. To be away from home and yet to feel oneself everywhere at home; to see the world, to be at the center of the world, and yet to remain hidden from the world." Charles Baudelaire, *The Painter of Modern Life and Other Essays*, trans. and ed., Jonathan Mayne (London: Phaidon, 1964), p. 9.
4. It is no accident that the postcard is one of the central emblems of his art. Concerning the element of tourism in his work, Alÿs says that "because I never really belong to cities, I try to invent a role for myself." In one photograph, he stands among Zócalo day laborers whose painted signs—plumber, locksmith—indicate their trades; Alÿs's sign reads "Turista." He also says of the postcards, "More than the image, it is the instructions on the cards that carry the story or plot. The action is something you can take with you, it can be 'stolen' then repeated verbally, like a fable or a rumor that might acquire a life of its own."
5. Alÿs's interest in animals in his own art is by no means restricted to the faithful, tenacious canine. The video *Cuentos Patrias* (1997), pictures him leading a flock of sheep around the Zócalo. In addition to the biblical resonances of this gesture, Alÿs was also alluding to the very public demonstrations in which Mexico's ruling PRI could mobilize its sheepish followers and paid party workers (and he unconsciously anticipated the enormously popular counter-demonstration in the same square led by the Zapatista resistance movement in 2001). For his entry, *The Ambassador*, in the 2001 Venice *Biennale*, he submitted a live peacock. "Mr. Peacock will represent Mr. Alÿs at the XLIX Biennale di Venezia," attendees were informed by postcard. The prancing, colorful "ambassador," who wandered around the Giardini and various national pavilions, raised questions about the age-old relationship between art and nature, mimicked the artist's own practice of walking, and deflated the pretensions of the art world at its most glamorous, self-important event.
6. Alÿs suggests that he is "trying to render the cyclical quality of history, the looping irony of human odyssey. It is more a phenomen[on] of pure present that captures me than a feeling of historical perspective. . . . I am obsessed with finding that moment of coincidence in between the experience of living and the consciousness of existence."

Francis Alÿs

1959 - Born in Antwerp
Lives and works in Mexico City

Selected One-Person Exhibitions

2001 - Antibes, France, Musée Picasso, *Francis Alÿs*, Apr. 14–June 17. Catalogue.
- London, Lisson Gallery, May 16–June 30.
- Zurich, Galerie Peter Kilchmann, *Francis Alÿs*, June 2–July 13.
- Hartford, Conn., Wadsworth Atheneum, *Francis Alÿs: MATRIX 145*, Oct. 6, 2001–Jan. 6, 2002. Brochure.

2000 - Montreal, Canada, Galerie de l'Université de Québec à Montréal, *The Last Clown*, Mar. 3–Apr. 8. Catalogue. Traveled to Winnepeg, Canada, Plug In Institute of Contemporary Art, May 5–24; Barcelona, Spain, Sala Moncada, Fundació la Caixa, June 16–July 23.
- Los Angeles, Acme, *Francis Alÿs*, Nov. 18–Dec. 23.

1999 - New York, www.diacenter.org, *The Thief*, Web project launched Mar. 11.
- Girona, Spain, Galería Mario Flecha, *Algunas veces, el hascer algo no lleva a nada/Cuentos patrioticos*, Aug. 10–30.
- Zurich, Galerie Peter Kilchmann, *Time Is a Trick of the Mind*, Aug. 28–Oct. 2.
- London, Lisson Gallery, *Stand-By*, Dec. 12, 1999–Jan. 29, 2000.

1998 - Vancouver, Canada, Contemporary Art Gallery, *Francis Alÿs: Le temps du sommeil*, July 4–Aug. 8. Catalogue. Traveled to Portland, Oreg., Portland Institute of Contemporary Art, Aug. 27–Oct. 4. Brochure.
- Vancouver, Canada, Or Gallery, *Dog Rose*, July 4–Aug. 1.

1997 - New York, Jack Tilton Gallery, *Le temps du sommeil*, Oct. 7–Nov. 1.
- Mexico City, Museo de Arte Moderno, *El mentiroso y la copia del mentiroso*, Nov. 27, 1997–Mar. 15, 1998.

1996 - Oaxaca, Mexico, Museo de Arte Contemporaneo de Oaxaca, *Francis Alÿs*, Feb. 9–Mar. 16.
- Los Angeles, Acme, *This Is My World*, Nov. 21–Dec. 21.

1995 - Ghent, Belgium, Opus Operandi, *Francis Alÿs*, Jan. 14–Feb. 19.

- New York, Jack Tilton Gallery, *The Liar: The Copy of the Liar*, Feb. 15–Mar. 11.
- São Paulo, Galeria Camargo Vilaça, *Other Peoples, Cities, Other Peoples, Work*, Aug. 2–26. Catalogue.

1994 - Guadalajara, Arena México Arte Contemporaneo, *The Liar: The Copy of the Liar*, September. Catalogue. Traveled to Monterrey, Mexico, Galería Ramis Barquet, October.

Selected Group Exhibitions

2001 - Minneapolis, Walker Art Center, *Painting at the Edge of the World*, Feb. 10–May 6. Catalogue.
- Paris, Musée d'Art Moderne de la Ville de Paris, *De adversidad vivemos*, June 1–Sept. 30. Catalogue.
- Bern, Museum of Fine Arts, *Black Box: The Dark Room in Art*, June 15–Dec. 9. Catalogue.
- Rotterdam, Witte de With/Center for Contemporary Art, *Squatters #1*, July 15–Sept. 23. Traveled to Porto, Portugal, Museu de Serralves, June 23–Sept. 30.
- Istanbul, Seventh Istanbul *Biennial*, Sept. 22–Nov. 17. Catalogue.
- New York, PS 1 Contemporary Art Center, *Animations*, Oct. 14, 2001–Jan. 13, 2002.

2000 - Rotterdam, *29th Rotterdam International Film Festival*, Jan. 29–Feb. 6.
- Dundee, Scotland, Dundee Contemporary Arts Center, *Dream Machines* (organized by the Hayward Gallery), Feb. 5–Mar. 26. Catalogue. Traveled to Sheffield, England, Mappin Art Gallery, July 8–Aug. 20; London, Camden Arts Centre, Sept. 7–Oct. 29.
- Lake Worth, Fla., Palm Beach Institute of Contemporary Art, *Making Time: Considering Time as a Material in Film and Video*, Mar. 5–May 28. Catalogue. Traveled to Los Angeles, UCLA Hammer Museum, Feb. 4–Apr. 22.
- Chicago, Museum of Contemporary Art, *Age of Influence: Reflections in the Mirror of American Culture*, Mar. 14–Dec. 26.
- Lucerne, Kunstmuseum Luzern, *Mixing Memory and Desire*, June 20–Sept. 24. Catalogue.
- Helsingör, Sweden, First Kulturbro *Biennial*, Sept. 16–Nov. 15. Catalogue.
- Antibes, France, Musée Picasso, *Un siècle d'arpenteurs, les figures de la mare*, Nov. 4, 2000–Jan. 14, 2001. Catalogue. Traveled to

San Sebastián, Spain, Koldo Mitxelena Kulturunea, Feb. 28–Apr. 21, 2001.

1999 - Annandale-on-Hudson, N.Y., Center for Curatorial Studies, Bard College, *Rewriting the City*, May 9–23. Brochure.
- Melbourne, *First International Melbourne Biennial*, May 11–June 11. Catalogue.
- Venice, 48th Venice *Biennale*, June 13–Nov. 7. Catalogue.
- Istanbul, Sixth Istanbul *Biennial*, Sept. 17–Oct. 30. Catalogue.
- Barcelona, Fundació Joan Miró, *La realitat i el desig*, Sept. 22–Nov. 7. Catalogue.
- Umeå, Sweden, Bildmuseet, *Mirror's Edge*, Nov. 21, 1999–Feb. 20, 2000. Catalogue. Traveled to Vancouver, Canada, Vancouver Art Gallery, Mar. 18–Aug. 13, 2000; Torino, Castello di Rivoli, Oct. 5, 2000–Jan. 14, 2001; Glasgow, Tramway, Mar. 2–Apr. 15, 2001; Copenhagen, Charlottenborg Undstillings-bygning, June 20–Aug. 26, 2001.

1998 - Caracas, Museo de Bellas Artes, *3. Bienal Barro de America*, May 31–July 5. Catalogue.
- London, Serpentine Gallery, *Loose Threads*, Aug. 22–Sept. 20. Catalogue.
- São Paulo, *24. Bienal Internacional de São Paulo*, Oct. 4–Dec. 13. Catalogue.
- Cambridge, England, Kettle's Yard (organized by Hayward Gallery, London), *Thinking Aloud*, Nov. 7, 1998–Jan. 3, 1999. Traveled to Manchester, Cornerhouse, Jan. 9–Feb. 28, 1999; London, Camden Arts Centre, Apr. 9–May 30, 1999.
- Mexico City, Museo de la Ciudad, *Cinco Continentes y una Ciudad: Segundo salon internacionale pintura*, Nov. 26, 1998–Feb. 28, 1999. Catalogue.

1997 - London, Whitechapel Art Gallery, *Antechamber*, Mar. 21–May 18. Exhibition guide.
- Tijuana; San Diego, Instituto Nacional de Bellas Artes; Installation Gallery, *InSite '97*, Sept. 26–Oct. 30. Catalogue.
- Deurle, Belgium, Museum Dhondt-Dhaenens, *Addenda*, Oct. 12–Dec. 7. Catalogue.

1996 - Boulder, Colo., Boulder Museum of Contemporary Art, *The Counterfeit Subject*, Mar. 1–May 5.
- Humlebaek, Denmark, Louisiana Museum of Modern Art, *NowHere*, May 15–Sept. 9. Catalogue.

- Graz, Austria, Sterischer Herbst, *Inclusion/Exclusion*, Sept. 11–Oct. 26.

1995 - Santa Fe, Site Santa Fe, *First International Biennial*, July 14–Oct. 8. Catalogue.

1994 - Havana, Centro Wifredo Lam, Fifth Havana *Bienal*, May 6–June 30. Catalogue.

adox of Praxis, Mexico City, 1997.

Sometimes making something leads to nothing.

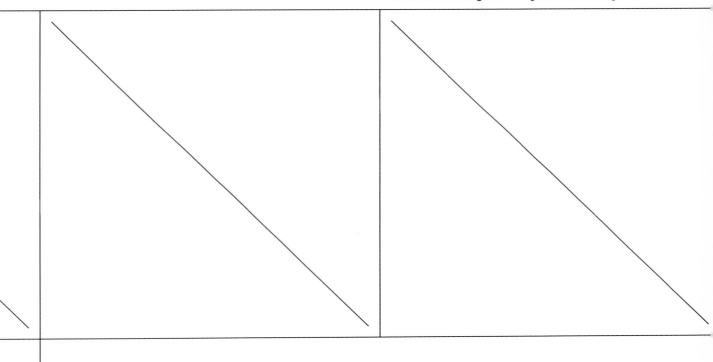

Having left the gallery, I wander through the neighborhoods carrying a leaking can of paint. My dripping action ends when, having found my way back to the gallery, thanks to my previous paint marks, I hang the empty can on the wall of the exhibition space. This story is an attempt to illustrate the contradictions of my practice.

The Leak, São Paolo, 1995.

(moderato) A. & B. arrive at opposite ends of Venice. A. is carrying the upper part of a tuba helicon, B. is carrying the lower part.

(andante) A. & B. wander through the city looking for each other.

(crescendo) Upon meeting, A. will help B. to reassemble the tuba.

(vibrato) With one breath, B. will play a note for as long as he can. A. will clap for as long as he can hold his breath.

Duet, Venice, 1999.

Sleepers II, Mexico City, 2001. Slide projection.

For an indeterminate period of time, the magnetized collector takes a daily walk through the streets and gradually builds up a coat made of any metallic residue lying in its path. This process goes on until the collector is completely covered by its trophies.

The Collector, Mexico City, 1991–92.

Francis Alÿs

To celebrate the moving of
the Museum of Modern Art from
its 53rd Street location to
MoMAQNS, to welcome MoMA's
masterpieces into the borough
of Queens, come and join the
Modern Procession on. . . .…

New York City, June . . . 2002

icon #1

punch

fireworks

camera

horse guard

MoMA 53rd St.

MoMA Queens →

horse guard

rose petals
& soap bubbles

icon #3

brass band

icon #2

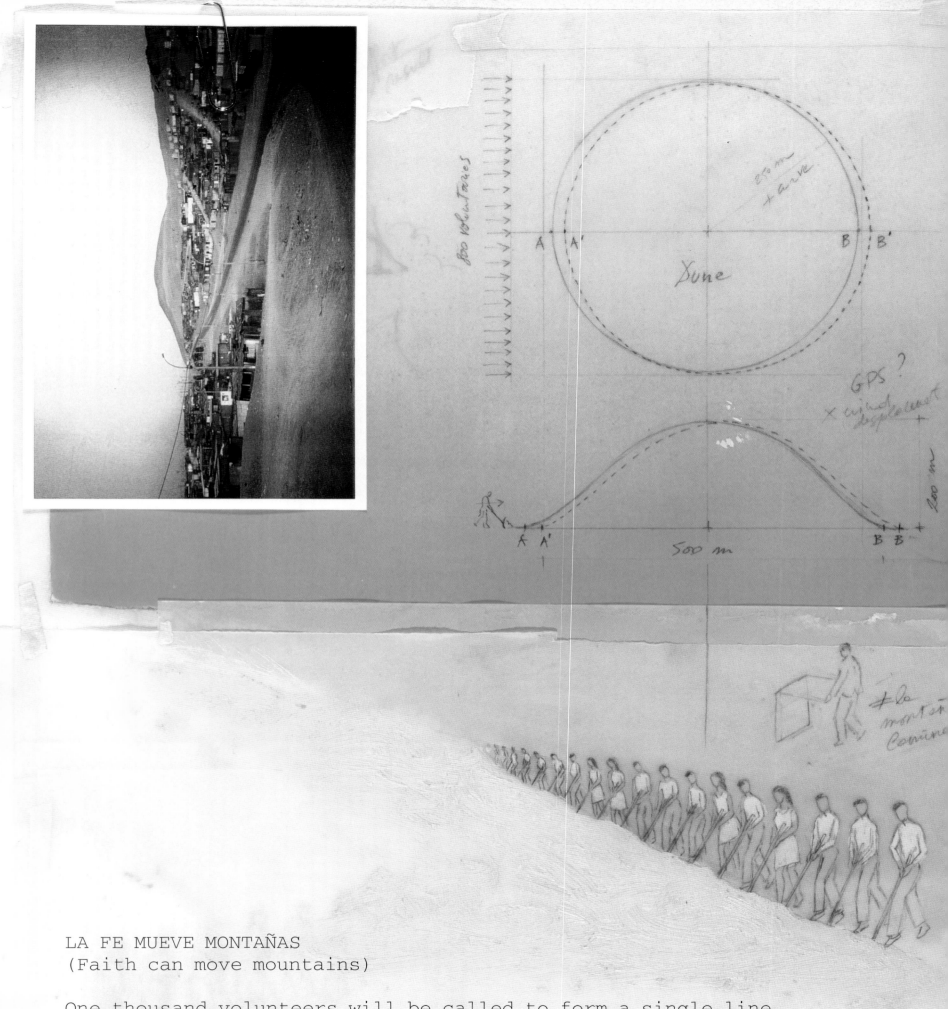

LA FE MUEVE MONTAÑAS
(Faith can move mountains)

One thousand volunteers will be called to form a single line,
equipped with shovels, and asked to produce the linear geological displacement of a 500-meter-long sand dune located
on the outskirts of the city of Lima. The actual shift will
be of an infinitesimal proportion, but not its metaphorical
resonance.

Lima, Peru, April 11, 2002

WALKING A PAINTING
London, January 2000
Trial for L.A., April 2002

- a painting* is hung
  on the museum** wall.
- as the museum opens its doors,
  the carrier takes the painting
  off the wall and walks the
  painting through the city.
- as night and closing time
  approach, the carrier brings
  the painting back to the
  museum, hangs it on the wall
  and covers it with a veil for
  the painting to sleep.
- the same actions are repeated
  the following day.

*painting: oil on canvas, wooden frame/62 x 120 x 10 cm
theme: "Across South L.A., blacks, whites, Latinos and
Asians are meeting in violent confrontations. The
popular myth that Los Angeles was transforming itself
into an harmonious multiethnic model city seems to waft
away in the smoke billowing over the city."
                          Los Angeles Times, April 30, 1992

**museum: as storage for collective memory and
  logistical base.

The filming begins at dawn with the flag-raising ceremony
and ends at dusk with the descending of the flag. The camera
follows the progression of the shadow of the flagpole and
the subsequent displacement of the people over the course
of the day. The camera lens describes a lateral movement
of 3 degrees per hour, for a total of 36 degrees/12 hours.

Zócalo, Mexico, D.F. May 20, 1999

The Mobility of the Real: Olafur Eliasson is Now

James Rondeau

There is, beneath these sharply cut crystals and this frozen surface, a continuous flux which is not comparable to any flux I have ever seen. There is a succession of states, each of which announces that which follows and contains that which precedes it. . . . Thus to seek with ready-made concepts to penetrate into the innermost nature of things is to apply to the mobility of the real a method created in order to give stationary points of observation on it. . . . Is it astonishing that, like children trying to catch smoke by closing their hands, philosophers so often see the object they would grasp fly before them?"

Henri Bergson, *An Introduction to Metaphysics,* 1903

Writing at the beginning of the twentieth century, Bergson's playful but melancholy description of a child's futile efforts to contain the ineffable offers a useful, if deceptively naive, metaphor for Olafur Eliasson's poetical approach to art making. Using landscape as the primary referent, Eliasson is engaged in a quasi-systematic study of human perception, or apprehension, of natural phenomena. The Danish-born artist has established a leading, international reputation for his photographs, sculptures, and installation-based works—all of which have been distinguished by a clever economy of means and a quiet, elegant beauty. As both an artist and amateur scientist, Eliasson demonstrates that sublime effect can indeed be captured by means of simple, pragmatic, mechanical actions or interventions. In our increasingly virtual age of hyper-mediated relationships to time and space, his sincere pursuit of beauty is itself remarkable. His work comes from a sense of genuine optimism, a modest but assured self-confidence, a belief in pleasure and play, and a canny sense of humor. It emerges from a place not unlike the one occupied by the smoke-catchers in Bergson's imagination.

Ultimately, however, Eliasson's deeply intelligent work allows a more familiar, postmodern skepticism. Produced with a combination of organic and synthetic materials, his art exists in an indeterminate border space between magic and artifice, romantic aspiration and artless imitation. Often, the artist's works are further inflected by self-consciously sentimental, vaguely melancholic titles, some of which suggest private narratives and longings: for example, *I grew up in solitude and silence* (1993); *Some people remember they were on the road that night* (1994); *A description of a reflection, or rather a pleasant exercise in its properties* (1995); *Your strange certainty still kept* (1996); *Tell me about a miraculous invention,* (1996); *Your foresight endured* (1996); *Your circumspection disclosed* (1999); *Your double diary* (1999); *Your blue afterimage exposed* (2000); and *The only thing we have in common is that we are different* (2000). With great linguistic and visual acumen, Eliasson insists that our present-day experience of the natural world is necessarily negotiated by a set of preexisting associations ranging from the emotional to the technological. By exposing these mediating factors, and staging nature on the level of what he calls "hyper-representation," Eliasson aims to create a more concentrated, more intense—one could even say, more real—experience of wonder.

As a photographer, Eliasson documents natural occurrences, oftentimes more aberrant than typical, such as icebergs, caves, rock formations, and islands. His serial images are presented in a straightforward grid arrangement, inviting comparisons and permitting the viewer to detect changes over time. With these landscape images (taken almost exclusively in Iceland), Eliasson is interested in both human time (e.g., ice melting) and geological time (e.g., glaciers moving). In all cases, the artist positions the representation of nature not as a conventional invitation to passive or even revelatory contemplation but as the catalyst for systematic study and investigation. In many ways, Eliasson's photographic practice serves as a point of departure, or as a kind of preliminary sketch, for his more compelling, installation-based works. (It is worth noting that the artist rarely chooses to exhibit these two distinct aspects of his production together.) Eliasson's indoor and outdoor installations are composed almost exclusively of ephemeral, immaterial elements: water (liquid and frozen), light, wind, fire, heat, fog, rainbows, magnetic waves, and the like. In some instances, these works rely on more tangible natural materials such as trees, thorns, moss, and grass. Given the profoundly spatial and temporal qualities of his chosen mediums, his installations are better understood as events (or presentations, demonstrations, experiments, incidents, etc.) than as sculptures in the conventional sense.

Eliasson is of Icelandic descent, was born and raised in Denmark, lives in Berlin, and works all over the world. The artist's relationship to Iceland is substantial: he spent a significant portion of his childhood and adolescence with family there, and has returned often as an adult. Since Eliasson first achieved international prominence in the mid 1990s, a great deal of critical attention has been paid to his Nordic roots. Indeed, much of the work has been read in an oversimplified relation to the landscape and geography of a place that is often referred to, somewhat mistakenly, as "his native Iceland." Eliasson has stated: "When I lived in Denmark, my Scandinavian identity was never an issue for me. When I left Scandinavia for Germany in 1993, I realized for the first time that the place you come from makes a difference. . . it did make me aware that my interests, at least historically, could be traced to the Scandinavian tradition." [1] Although the artist has been quick to acknowledge his relationship to a Nordic landscape tradition, the repeated emphasis on his national identity—particularly in regard to the exotic appeal of Iceland's dramatic, desolate landscape—has begun to over determine other critical (i.e. more theoretical than biographical) readings of his work: "The importance of my national identity has always been dramatically exaggerated by critics and art historians who tend to use it as a shortcut for interpretations of my work. Basically, I consider myself Scandinavian or northern European. I don't mind talking about it since it's no secret where I am from. I can say, however, that there is nothing mystical about coming from Iceland." [2] In fact, Eliasson's formal concerns can be just as readily linked to the history of art as they can to the geography of his childhood. Of particular relevance to an understanding of his work are the so-called California "light and space" artists Robert Irwin, Maria Nordman, and James Turrell. Irwin's architectural installations with translucent scrims and Nordman's pioneering experiments with direct and reflected sunlight seemingly have a special resonance with Eliasson's practice, although he had no direct exposure to these works as a student. In fact, the differences between his practice and its antecendents—which are in part generational differences—are more instructive than the similarities. Many of Eliasson's light and space predecessors, Turrell in particular, were interested in using light to achieve a sort of trompe l'oeil Minimalism. Never sure of what they are seeing or not seeing, viewers of a Turrell light installation, for example, are intentionally confronted and confused by spatial ambiguities, optical illusions, and sometimes even total darkness. Eliasson's works, in sharp contrast, are simple, direct, and immediately comprehensible. For example, when he installed *Your sun machine* (1997), at the Marc Foxx gallery in Los Angeles, he simply cut a hole in the gallery ceiling and allowed the bright California sun to shine into the space. Eliasson's "sculpture" was visible as an isolated patch of light, moving across the floor in the same path during the course of each day. In another important early work, *Your strange certainty still kept* (1996), Eliasson secured a roof gutter to a gallery ceiling and used a needle to puncture tiny holes in a garden hose attached along the top of the gutter. Water fell from the ceiling into a long basin below and then was pumped back up to the roof gutter. With a flashing strobe light cast at an oblique angle to the piece, Eliasson created the appearance of water drops suspended in midair.

The result was a luminous curtain of light and water floating in space, and a full spectral rainbow reflected on the floor.

These and other works are assembled from decidedly low-tech and readily available components; the artist makes no attempt to conceal the apparatus producing the effect. The rudimentary technology he employs—hoses, electric lights, extensions cords, water pumps, scaffolding, or whatever is required to make the piece—is always immediately visible upon entering Eliasson's spaces. There are no secrets, no slick tricks—only spatial situations designed, as the artist says, to help us "sense ourselves sensing."

By isolating effects that mirror or reproduce natural phenomena within the context of spaces devoted to art and aesthetics, Eliasson focuses and intensifies the sensory aspects of the experience. One of the artist's definitive works in this regard is *Waterfall* (1998), a rudimentary, freestanding construction of scaffolding, plastic, aluminum, and wood, which was first installed in the Botanical Gardens in Sydney, Australia. The towering assemblage is activated by a water pump that sends thousands of gallons of water per second through a large hose into a basin positioned atop the scaffolding some two stories high. A curtain of water cascades down the full height of the structure, collects in a similar basin just above the ground, and then is immediately recycled back, or up, into the piece. With *Waterfall*, Eliasson ingeniously reveals that both the affect and the effect of the work are not qualitatively different, in any meaningful way, from the experience of a naturally occurring waterfall. The drama of falling water, the crashing sound of the falls, the reflection of light in the water, the misty dampness of the surrounding air, and so on—all of these elements are tangibly present. The viewer is not confronted with a representation or even an approximation, of a waterfall. Instead, Eliasson presents an essentialized waterfall that is at once manufactured and real, perhaps even more real than its referent in a forest. With works like this, the artist simultaneously creates and recontextualizes (or displaces), abstracts, and intensifies the actuality of the experience by locating it in a space (or as part of a larger project) devoted to contemporary art, as opposed to say, outdoor recreation.

"Nature" is deployed in Eliasson's work not as an end in itself but as a means to investigate individual subjectivity. The real subject of his work is ultimately the skills of perception that reside within each viewer. The poetics of his titles, along with the artist's now signature use of a second-person possessive pronoun, points to the centrality of the individual viewer in Eliasson's conception of his larger project. One of the artist's most useful, and persistent, formulations comes in the form of the title for his 2000 installation at the Art Institute of Chicago: *Your intuitive surroundings versus your surrounded intuition*. This title refers to the environment versus the viewer within the environment. In the logic of this challenging wordplay, surroundings are surrounded and the surrounded is placed within viewers' surroundings. Eliasson positions us as viewers in an emphatically present tense, both as subject and object of his work. Sometimes, he imagines that the usual rules of spectatorship have been reversed, and the object or environment is actually looking at the viewer. Eliasson's work, in that regard, can be understood in the most basic sense as a platform, an environment designed for a generous, complex, and calm examination of our seeing, thinking, and being.

1 Olafur Eliasson, quoted in Francesco Bonami, "Psychological Atmospheres," *Siksi: The Nordic Art Review* 12, no. 3 (autumn 1997), p. 55.
2 Eliasson, in conversation with the author.

Olafur Eliasson

1967 - Born in Copenhagen
Lives and works in Berlin

Selected One-Person Exhibitions

2002 - Paris, Musée d'Art Moderne de la Ville de Paris, *Olafur Eliasson: Chaque matin, je me sens different*, Mar. 22–May 12. Catalogue
- Reykjavík, i8 Galleri, *Yet Untitled*, May 12–June 22.
- Munich, Kunstbau Lenbachhaus, *Olafur Eliasson*, Sept. 7, 2002–Jan. 2003. Catalogue.

2001 - Boston, The Institute of Contemporary Art, *Your Only Real Thing Is Time*, Jan. 24–Apr. 1. Catalogue.
- Bregenz, Austria, Kunsthaus Bregenz, *The Mediated Motion*, Mar. 23–May 13. Catalogue.
- Karlsruhe, Zentrum für Kunst und Medientechnologie, *Surroundings Surrounded*, May 31–Aug. 26. Catalogue.
- New York, The Museum of Modern Art, *Seeing Yourself Sensing*, Sept. 13, 2001–May 21, 2002. Brochure.
- Berlin, Neugerriemschneider, *Die Dinge die du nicht siehst, die du nicht siehst*, Nov. 3–Dec. 15. Catalogue.
- Ljubljana, Moderna Galerija, *The Structural Evolution Project*, Nov. 22, 2001–Jan. 6, 2002.

2000 - Dublin, Irish Museum of Modern Art, *The Curious Garden*, Jan. 19–Apr. 30. Catalogue.
- Ridgefield, Conn., Aldrich Museum of Contemporary Art, *Olafur Eliasson: New Work*, Jan. 23–Apr. 30. Catalogue.
- Kitakyushu, Japan, Center for Contemporary Art, *The Only Thing We Have in Common Is That We Are Different*, Feb. 21–Mar. 10.
- Tokyo, Masataka Hayakawa Gallery, *Your Blue Afterimage Exposed*, Feb. 24–Mar. 25. Brochure.
- Tokyo, Gallery Koyanagi, *Your Orange Afterimage Exposed*, Feb. 24–Mar. 25.
- Graz, Neue Galerie Graz, *Surrounding Surrounded*, Apr. 1–May 21. Catalogue.
- Chicago, The Art Institute, *Your Intuitive Surroundings versus Your Surrounded Intuition*, May 10–Aug. 13. Catalogue.
- Wolfsburg, Germany, Kunstverein Wolfsburg, *Highlighter*, May 31–June 11.
- Stockholm, International Artists Studio Program, *Syndrome 2*, Sept. 1–24. Catalogue.

- New York, Bonakdar Jancou Gallery, *Your Now Is My Surroundings*, Oct. 24–Dec. 2.

1999 - Santa Monica, Marc Foxx, Jan. 9–Feb. 6.
- Milan, Emi Fontana, *Riflessi di una certa importanza*, Feb. 11–Mar. 16.
- Turin, Castello di Rivoli, *Your Circumspection Disclosed*, Mar. 24–May 23. Catalogue.
- Wolfsburg, Germany, Kunstverein Wolfsburg, *Your Circumspection Disclosed*, May 11–June 20. Catalogue.
- Dundee, Scotland, Dundee Contemporary Arts, *Your Position Surrounded and Your Surroundings Positioned*, Sept. 18–Nov. 7. Catalogue.

1998 - Zurich, Galerie Peter Kilchmann, *A Cycle of Softening and the Assisted View*, Jan. 24–Mar. 14.
- Reykjavík, Reykjavík Art Museum, *The Parallel Garden and Other Stories*, Mar. 7–Apr. 13. Catalogue.
- Umeå, Sweden, Bildmuseet, *Olafur Eliasson: Fotografier/ Photoworks*, Mar. 15–Apr. 12. Catalogue.
- New York, Tanya Bonakdar Gallery, *The Inventive Velocity versus Your Inverted Veto*, Apr. 30–June 4.
- Kiel, Germany, Galerie Enja Wonnenberger, *Aquarium*, May 13–June 20.
- Aarhus, Denmark, Aarhus Kunstmuseum, *Tell Me about a Miraculous Invention*, Aug. 29–Oct. 18. Catalogue.
- Berlin, Neugerriemschneider, *Yet Untitled*, Sept. 8–25.
- Leipzig, Galerie für Zeitgenössische Kunst Leipzig, Nov. 8–Dec. 6. Catalogue.
- Reykjavík, i8 Galleri, Dec. 9, 1998–Jan. 10, 1999.

1997 - Basel, Kunsthalle Basel, *The Curious Garden*, Jan. 19–Feb. 23. Catalogue.
- Copenhagen, Stalke Galeri, *New Photos by Olafur Eliasson*, Apr. 11–May 17. Catalogue.
- Santa Monica, Calif., Marc Foxx, Apr. 26–May 31.

1996 - New York, Tanya Bonakdar Gallery, *Your Strange Certainty Still Kept*, Apr. 27–May 25.
- Stockholm, Galeri Andreas Brändström, *Tell Me about a Miraculous Invention*, May 4–May 29.
- Milan, Emi Fontana, *Your Foresight Endured*, Sept. 24–Nov. 31.
- Malmö, Kunstmuseet, Oct. 19–Nov. 30.

1995 - Odense, Denmark, Tommy Lund Galerie, *Olafur Eliasson*, March.
- Hamburg, Hamburger Kunstverein, *Thoka*, Apr. 22–May 28.
- Stuttgart, Künstlerhaus, *Olafur Eliasson*, September.
- Berlin, Neugerriemschneider, *A Description of a Reflection, or a Pleasant Exercise Regarding Its Qualities*, Nov. 4–Dec. 22.

1994 - Malmö, Forumgallereit, *Olafur Eliasson*, January.
- Cologne, Lukas and Hoffmann, *Olafur Eliasson*, October.
- Copenhagen, Stalke Galerie, *Lilja Lever*, Dec. 2, 1994–Jan. 12, 1995. Catalogue.

Selected Group Exhibitions

2001 - Bern, Museum of Fine Arts, *Black Box: The Dark Room in Art*, June 15–Dec. 9. Catalogue.
- Yokohama, First Yokohama Triennial, Sept. 2–Nov. 11. Catalogue.
- Washington, D.C., Corcoran Gallery of Art, *Confronting Nature*, Oct. 13–Nov. 26. Catalogue.

2000 - London, Serpentine Gallery, *The Greenhouse Effect*, Apr. 4–May 21. Catalogue.
- Graz, International Garden Show: *The Magic Garden*, Apr. 13–Oct. 15.
- St. Louis, St. Louis Museum of Art, *Wonderland*, July 1–Sept. 24. Catalogue.
- Humlebaek, Denmark, Louisiana Museum of Modern Art, *Vision and Reality: Conceptions of the Twentieth Century*, Sept. 21, 2000–Jan. 14, 2001. Catalogue.

1999 - Cambridge, Mass., Massachusetts Institute of Technology List Visual Arts Center, *Landscape: Outside the Frame*, Apr. 23–June 27. Catalogue.
- Venice, 48th Venice *Biennale*, June 13–Nov. 7. Catalogue.
- Amsterdam, De Appel Foundation, *Job Koelewijn and Olafur Eliasson*, June 18–Aug. 22.
- Münster, *Skulptur. Projekte in Münster*, Aug. 7–Sept. 27. Catalogue.
- Pittsburgh, Carnegie Museum of Art, *Carnegie International*, Nov. 6, 1999–Mar. 26, 2000. Catalogue.
- New York, PS 1 Contemporary Art Center, *Children of Berlin*, Nov. 7, 1999–Jan. 2, 2000. Catalogue.

1998 - Moss, Norway, Momentum, May 23–June 21. Catalogue.
- Sydney, *11th Biennial of Sydney*, Sept. 18–Nov. 8. Catalogue.
- Berlin, First Berlin *Biennial*, Sept. 30, 1998–Jan. 8, 1999. Catalogue.
- Vilnius, Lithuania, Contemporary Art Center, *Seventh Baltic Triennial of Contemporary Art*, Oct. 1–Nov. 2. Catalogue.
- São Paulo, *24. Bienal Internacional de São Paulo*, Oct. 4–Dec. 13. Catalogue.

1997 - Santa Fe, Site Santa Fe, *Second International Biennial*, July 18–Oct. 12. Catalogue.
- Istanbul, Fifth Istanbul *Biennial*, Oct. 4–Nov. 9. Catalogue.
- Johannesburg, Second Johannesburg *Biennial*, Oct. 10–Dec. 18. Catalogue.

1996 - Frankfurt, Frankfurter Kunstverein, *Prospect '96*, Mar. 9–May 12. Catalogue.
- Rotterdam, *Manifesta 1*, June 9–Aug. 19. Catalogue.

1995 - Venice, Corderie dell'Arsenale, *Campo '95*, June 7–July 30. Traveled to Sant'Antonio di Susa, Italy, Palazzo Rebaudengo par l'Arte, Oct. 20–Dec. 31; Malmö, Konstmuseet, Feb. 11–Apr. 8, 1996. Catalogue.

Moss wall, 1994. Moss, dimensions variable.

Your sun machine, 1997. Hole in roof and sunlight, dimensions variable. Installation at Marc Foxx, Santa Monica, 1997. Collection Rena Conti and Dr. Ivan Moskowitz, Brookline, Mass.

...ur strange certainty still kept, 1996. Water, strobe lights, hose, ...exiglas, pump, and wood. Installation at Tanya Bonakdar ...allery, New York, 1996. Collection Dakis Joannou, Athens.

Waterfall, 1998. Water, water pump, hose, aluminum, plastic, scaffolding, dimensions variable. Installation at Neue Galerie, Graz, 2000.

The double sunset, 1999. Aluminum and xenon lamps, dimensions variable. Installation in Utrecht, 1999.

Olafur Eliasson

Hachiya Kazuhiko: New Paradigm of Media Art

Yuko Hasegawa

I once heard about a robot bird, the result of a collaboration between an artist and an ecologist. The electronic creature was used as a navigator, guiding birds whose migratory habits and instincts had been undermined by environmental pollution and global warming.

To survive, we embark on new experiences that broaden our cognitive horizons. These processes also motivate artists and are the basic objectives to which Hachiya Kazuhiko aspires. Armed with experience in marketing, design, and technology, he both intrudes and expands on the traditional boundaries of art.

Some of Hachiya's ideas are based on physical interaction and play (he was a skilled gymnast and is a roller skater), and his methodology involves having others experiment and directly engage with those ideas. He believes in the possibilities of new synapses, convinced that "anyone can do a back somersault once the right connections are made in the brain."[1] Hachiya's works are capable of engaging all the senses. In 1992, he created the Reach/Unreach Suit, a "media suit" equipped with perception-enhancing devices such as goggles with built-in liquid crystal display monitors and a helmet with two video cameras and headphones, which record and amplify the wearer's movements. The initial participant was Hachiya, but the suit was conceived so that anyone could wear it. With each step, the video camera would record and emit the movement back to him in the form of a strobe light's flash, and a vibration would be felt throughout his body. In this experience and others like it, his ideas are intuited through the body and evolve from there.

While it is physically interactive, Hachiya's work is also designed to have a psychological effect. It often produces pleasure in the viewer and a sense of excited accomplishment similar to what one experiences when playing a computer game. Some of his works may even include sensual experiences. "Favorite," "delicious," and "visceral" are words often used to describe the ephemeral pleasures created by the information age. Yet when Hachiya speaks of experiential works, he is talking about maintaining the reality of pleasure and the political subtext he imposes on it by asking if a physical experience can criticize or revolt against the age in which we live.

The Engineering of Consciousness

Hachiya's work questions media technology as it functions in the broader social realm. It embraces two main themes: the first is the engineering of consciousness, and the second might be described as promoting a parallel world comprised of socially critical works.

Among the works addressing the first theme is *Inter Discommunication Machine* (1993/2002). It is the artist's fundamental belief that communication is impossible, and the inspiration for this work was his Freudian curiosity about the way he is viewed by his partner during sex. This fascination with the notion of looking at himself through the eyes of others also came to him as he swam with dolphins when he visited the Ogasawara Islands. During this trip, he studied the bionomics of dolphins and learned that they use the greater part of their cerebral cortex to communicate with each other. He believes that echolocation might even allow dolphins to share their visions. Hachiya's aim with *Inter Discommunication Machine* is to forge communication between two people who are temporarily deprived of their auditory and visual senses and thus forced to rely on one another's hearing and sight via head-mounted displays and transmitters equipped with antennae. If one participant fails to enter the other's field of vision, the two will never meet. This forced structure, whereby the search for and discovery of oneself comes through an encounter with another, distinguishes Hachiya's work from that of Vito Acconci and Bruce Nauman, who compel the spectator to confront an amplified sense of self-awareness.

Hachiya's *Vanishing Body*—made for the group exhibition *De-Genderism* at the Setagaya Art Museum, Tokyo, in 1997—

turned spectators into performers, transforming a familiar other into a stranger. Before entering a darkened semicircular space that was divided in two by a screen, participants were asked whether they wished to remove their clothing. Those who did were provided with Jagarandi, special eyewear developed by Hachiya, which allowed a participant to see the silhouette of another participant on the other side of the screen. Without the Jagarandi, nothing could be seen but darkness. The screen was elastic, permitting participants on opposite sides to touch each other if they wished to. The silhouettes glowed like aliens, and physical attributes such as gender or age were nullified. *Vanishing Body* was an attempt to (re)discover another being through communication in the dark. It eliminated the feeling of security viewers of artworks normally retain; those accepting the requirement of complete nudity were subjected to the alienation of being placed under observation and those rejecting it were alienated from the "viewing" experience.

A Parallel World

Hachiya's parallel world—a faint, warm vision of the future— is a fantasy that asks, What if evolution had proceeded along a different vector? It is also a warning bell that he is sounding to the present age. It is his way of criticizing the mindless pursuit of efficiency and rationalism, as well as making us aware of the human and emotional elements that slow the evolution of technology.

First developed in 1996, Hachiya's popular *PostPet* software transmits e-mail in the form of "pets" who are nothing more than binary data. A dancing pink bear named Momo was the first PostPet he created; now there are others, including Mini-Rabbit Mippi and Penguin Ushe. Each PostPet lives in its own room (an electronic space). It might go out to deliver e-mail and not return until the recipient picks up the message. Sometimes a PostPet sends e-mail to its owner or a frequent correspondent, either intentionally or acciden-

tally. It may get into arguments with someone else's PostPet who arrives bearing e-mail for its owner, and these arguments can turn into brawls. In an age when the prime attraction of e-mail is its efficiency and speed, the software that features these troublemakers has been used by several million people since Sony released it in Japan in 1997. Why is it so popular? Information-transmission tools—increasingly convenient, transparent, and expeditious—reduce the pleasure derived from genuine communication, and the transformation of the electronic environment into imagery—pets that live in the electronic space surrounding us—makes us more resistant to the stress brought on by computer problems and the risk of discommunication. Hachiya's concept is influenced by Japan's animistic cultural background, also evident in Pokémon and such films as Hayao Miyazaki's *Kaze no Tani no Naushika* (1984, released in English as *Warriors of the Wind*).

Thanks Tails (1996/2001) involve another level of social criticism. Hachiya views Japan's roads as barbaric battlefields, where every year 1,150,000 people are injured in traffic accidents and more than 10,000 are killed (a number including only those expiring on the same day as the accident). The *Thanks Tails* project involves affixing metal "dog tails" to the rear of automobiles, allowing the driver to produce gestures and signals, such as making the tail wag as a sign of thanks. Hachiya's goal is for three percent of the world's automobiles to be equipped with *Thanks Tails*. If he is successful, his social sculpture will transform the landscape.

The Spirituality of Technology

Hachiya's installation *World System*—made for the Japan Art Scholarship Grand Prix exhibition at Spiral Garden, Tokyo, 1995—was inspired by concepts developed by Serbian-American inventor Nikola Tesla. Involving wireless technology, the work was based on Tesla's concept of the wireless transmission of information and electricity. As Hachiya has described it, *World System* is a model of a flying video telephone that you fly up in search of, and connect to once you've located it. Driven by the energy created by six participants, the installation included six beds that moved back and forth, propelled gently by motors. While lying down on a bed, each person wore a special mask outfitted with camera, speakers, and microphone, which transmitted live information—the voices of other participants, images of the entire installation—to the wearer. Like Hachiya's Reach/Unreach Suit, the masks, and the beds themselves, transmitted the sensations of movement and sound directly to the participant's body, so he/she was aware of everyone else's breathing, speaking, and, essentially, their collective existence. The *World System* installation constituted a metaphorical experience during which each participant's "spirit" left his/her body and communicated with the others. This may be viewed as a romantic or somewhat nostalgic and imaginative interpretation of past scientific developments such as Tesla's. However, Hachiya's approach is not merely a (re)visioning of early technological devices—in fact, he is currently developing wireless telephone software.

Hachiya's ongoing *Mega Diary* project, which began in 1995, consists of diary entries posted to a Web site. Here, Hachiya expresses his opposition, in the simplest way possible, to the practice of reducing the dead to statistics. Suppose a fighter pilot, poised to drop a bomb, encounters a massive body of data in the form of a "mega diary," a compilation of entries posted to the Web by tens of thousands of individuals residing in the target zone. Having read them, can he bring himself to drop the bomb?

The ambivalence of Hachiya's world—in which intellectual and primitive emotions, human kindness and radicalism, ethics and anarchism, coexist—is generated by a process that incorporates technology and the artist's longstanding dialogue with his own body. This methodology—seeming at first glance like a child's simple posing of a question—permeates the consciousness, and the limbic system, of those who experience his work. In Hachiya's hands, technology takes on the character of spirituality.

Translated from the Japanese by Connie Prener.

1 Hachiya, in conversation with author.

Hachiya Kazuhiko

1966 - Born in Saga, Japan
       Lives and works in Tokyo

Selected One-Person Exhibitions

1999 - Tokyo, Gallery Art Soko, *Air Board Beta for the Jet Generation*, Sept. 4–12.

1996 - Hiroshima, Hiroshima City Museum of Contemporary Art, *Seeing Is Believing*, June 15–July 14. Brochure.

1995 - Tokyo, Spiral Garden, *The Fourth Japan Art Scholarship Grand Prix: Kazuhiko Hachiya World System*, Nov. 3–12.
       - Fukuoka, Mitsubishi-Jisho Artium, *Love Doubler*, Dec. 14, 1995–Jan. 15, 1996.

1994 - Tokyo, P3 Art and Environment, *Over the Rainbow*, July 7–25.

1993 - Tokyo, Roentgen Kunstinstitut von Katsuya Ikeuchi Galerie AG, *Inter Dis-Communication*, Aug. 6.

Selected Group Exhibitions

2002 - Tokyo, Tokyo Metropolitan Museum of Photography, *ReImagination: Image/Media/Museum*, Mar. 1–May 9.

2001 - London, Barbican Art Gallery, *JAM: Tokyo-London*, May 10–July 8. Catalogue. Traveled to Tokyo, Tokyo Opera City Art Gallery, Feb. 8–May 6, 2002.
       - Tokyo, Fuji Television Forum, *New York Philip Morris Art Award: 24 Winners from 1996 to 2000*, June 2–17. Catalogue. Traveled to Osaka, Umeda Stella Hall, June 23–July 1.
       - Istanbul, Seventh Istanbul *Biennial*, Sept. 22–Nov. 17. Catalogue.

2000 - Tokyo, Tepia, *Pastiche Fresh Whole: Milk with Site Scanner*, Mar. 2–4.
       - Tokyo, Museum of Contemporary Art Tokyo, *The Gift of Hope*, Dec. 16, 2000–Apr. 8, 2001. Catalogue.

1999 - New York, Grey Art Gallery, *The First Steps: Emerging Artists from Japan*, Jan. 29–Mar. 20. Catalogue.
       - Kyongju, Sonje Museum of Contemporary Art, *Fancy Dance*, July 2–Aug. 29. Catalogue.
       - Bonn, Kunstmuseum Bonn, *Zeitwenden: Ruckblick und Ausblick*, Dec. 4, 1999–June 4, 2000.

Catalogue. Traveled to Vienna, 20er Haus, July 5–Oct. 1, 2000.

1998 - Tokyo, Tokyo International Forum, *Philip Morris Art Award 1998*, June 30–July 10. Catalogue.
       - Linz, www.aec.at/festival/, *The Prix Ars Electronica '98*, Sept. 7–12. Catalogue.

1997 - Tokyo, Setagaya Art Museum, *De-Genderism: Détruire dit-elle/il*, Feb. 8–Mar. 23. Catalogue.
       - Budapest, Kiscelli Museum, *Dream of Existence: Young Japanese Artists*, Mar. 13–Apr. 13. Catalogue.
       - Paris, Créteil Maison des Arts, *Exit*, Mar. 29–30.
       - Linz, www.aec.at/festival/, *The Prix Ars Electronica '97*, Sept. 8–13. Catalogue.
       - Tokyo, Nadiff Gallery, *PostPet Ex*, Oct. 22–Nov. 19.
       - Fukui, Japan, Fukui City Art Museum, Seventh Fukui *Biennial*, Nov. 15–Dec. 7. Catalogue.

1996 - Shibukawa, Japan, Hara Museum of Contemporary Art, *Art Is Fun 7: In/Out*, July 6–Sept. 1. Catalogue.
       - Tokyo, Tokyo Big Sight, *On Camp/Off Base*, Aug. 10–19.
       - Linz, www.aec.at/festival/, *The Prix Ars Electronica '96*, Sept. 2–7. Catalogue.
       - Mito, Japan, Contemporary Art Gallery, Art Tower Mito, *Art Scene 90–96: Seeing Is Believing*, Nov. 30, 1996–Jan. 19, 1997. Catalogue.

1995 - Nagoya, Nagoya City Science Museum, *Artec '95: The Fourth International Biennial in Nagoya*, Apr. 28–June 25.
       - Osaka, Kirin Plaza Osaka, *New Asian Art Show*, July 20–Aug. 3. Catalogue. Traveled to Tokyo, Japan Foundation Forum, Aug. 23–Sept. 6.

1994 - Beijing, The Art Museum of Capital Normal University, *Com-Art Show*, Oct. 25–31.

1993 - Suwon, Korea, Jangan Park, *Com-Art Show*, Oct. 2–7.

1992 - Tokyo, Spiral Garden, *Third Video Television Festival*, Feb. 1–11.
       - Tokyo, Machida City Museum of Graphic Arts, *Video Art after Video Art*, Oct. 27–Nov. 22. Brochure.

Hachiya Kazuhiko

Inter Discommunication Machine, 1993/2002. Video camera transmitters, head mounted displays, batteries, and feathers. Installation at *The Prix Arts Electronica*, Linz, Austria, 1996.

Vanishing Body, 1997. Jagarandi eyewear, infrared light, elastic screen, and wood. Installation at Setagaya Art Museum, Tokyo, 1997.

PostPet, 1996–2002. Computer mailing software. Plan and direction by Hachiya Kazuhiko; graphics by Manabe Namie; programming and engineering by Koki Takashi.

nks Tails, 1996/2001. Aluminum, fiberglass reinforced stic, servo motor, and battery. Installed on automobile.

World System, 1995 (detail). Mixed media with motors, video cameras, head-mounted displays, beds, chairs, and daisies. Installation at Spiral Garden, Tokyo, 1995.

Hachiya Kazuhiko

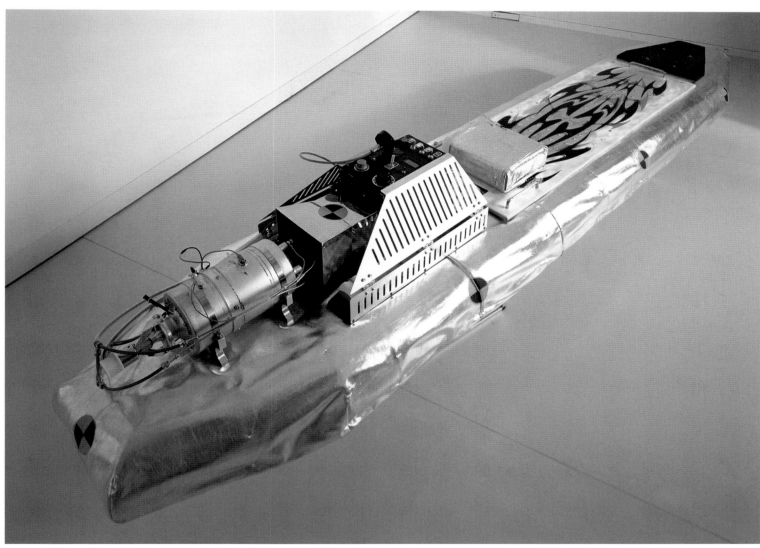

PostPet™
© Sony Communication Network Corpration.

PostPet（モモの部屋）

メールを書く

おともだち帳

受信簿

送信簿

メールチェック

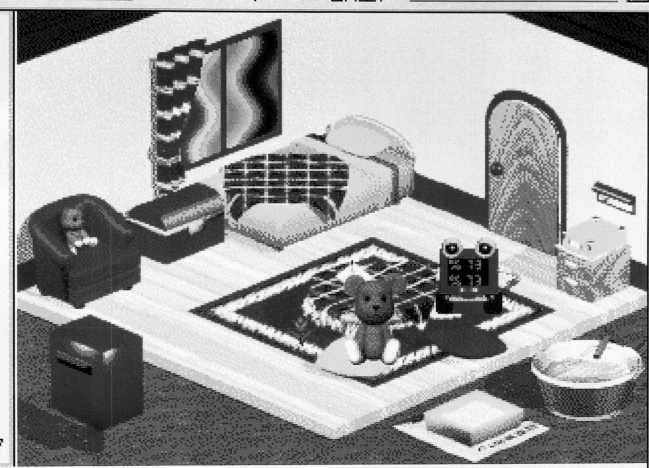

ママさんちのシンゴがきました。

Expansive Terrains: Pierre Huyghe

Maria-Christina Villaseñor

"At any given moment, fiction gives rise to reality," says Pierre Huyghe.[1] Upending the conventional wisdom of reality as inspiration for flights of fiction, he posits that the cinema and other texts can and do, equally in turn, give rise to an expanded reality. The movies and media have become our collective consciousness; their documentation and representation inform the lived experience of the present rather than simply offering nostalgic references to the past. The concepts of participation and engagement have shifted significantly since Bruce Nauman, Nam June Paik, Dan Graham, and company first explored video recording, playback, and issues of instantaneity in the 1960s and early 1970s. Expanding upon this media tradition, Huyghe questions definitions of experience, memory, and engagement in his installations, site-specific works, and community projects.

Huyghe often uses film as his primary source material. By extending filmic space through formal and conceptual strategies, he emphasizes the unlimited possibilities of interpretation and offers a resonate interactivity that functions on literal and metaphoric levels. In his works, cinema and the text become active spaces for the viewer's engagement rather than passive spaces of consumption. Whether the engagement for the viewer/participant is literal—for example, *Atari Light* (1999) and its invitation to a playful game or *Mobil TV* (1995–98) with its means for a community to broadcast its own stories and concerns—or metaphoric—*L'Ellipse* (1998) with its examination of the gap of a jump cut or *Dubbing* (1996) with the actors dubbing others and inserting themselves into a drama—Huyghe is less interested in structural rules than in the possibilities that result from bending them.

Perhaps nothing better illustrates Huyghe's manipulation of these rules than his installation *The Third Memory* (1999), which takes as its point of departure a crime in Brooklyn. Bank robber John Woytowicz's drama, which unfolded live in front of television viewers on August 22, 1972, is today more commonly recalled in its dramatized version: Sidney Lumet's film

Dog Day Afternoon (1975). For *The Third Memory* Huyghe tracked down the now portly and gray-haired Woytowicz in order to let him tell his own tale. The result is a third memory, neither the first memory as experienced by the participants and television viewers at the time the original event took place, nor the second memory as depicted by Al Pacino in the film. In Huyghe's installation, with two projections creating a split-screen effect, cameras stealthily move around Woytowicz as he directs actors, plays "himself," and addresses the viewer/camera to recount and reenact his version of the robbery. The footage of Woytowicz's reenactment must also compete at times with news footage and scenes from Lumet's film. Woytowicz's story is no longer his alone, and simplified notions of reality and fiction, the documentary and imaginary, are no longer possible. The psychological and cinematic projections, improvisations, and documented enactments and reenactments have intertwined so completely that they have produced a new, third memory.

Huyghe's expansive horizontal terrains call to mind Gilles Deleuze and Félix Guattari's concept of the rhizome, in which nonhierarchical systems allow for endless points of entry and mutations of meaning. Similarly, Huyghe expands upon French cinematic terminology. In his works, "doublage," meaning sound dubbing, evokes the more resonant "doubling." "Voix-off," meaning voice-over, suggests a voice or presence that exists in a ghostly space "off," or outside, the film frame. "Ellipse," meaning jump cut, suggests ellipsis, or an omission. "Travelling," meaning tracking, evokes the broader sense of traveling in the world at large. And "acteur," meaning the interpreter of a role, also means the agent who effectuates change. His application of such terminology—not only as words but also as techniques—underscores the generous expanse of the imaginary that he grants viewers as active interpreters and producers of meaning.

L'Ellipse makes use of Wim Wenders's *The American Friend* (1977), a film that typifies that director's laconically meandering style, in which empty space, a journey, sounds, and music articulate the characters as much or more so than any dialogue or dramatic actions. In the triple-projection installation of *L'Ellipse*, projections to the right and left show scenes from *The American Friend* on either sides of a jump cut: on the right, the film's protagonist, played by Bruno Ganz, gets a phone call and is told to meet the caller at another building, visible from his window; on the left, Ganz is in a room at the other location. The installation's middle segment, also featuring Ganz, presents Huyghe's newly filmed musing on the "space" in between the two scenes. Ganz, though noticeably older than in his 1977 performance, seamlessly moves through the disjointed temporal yet contiguous space of the original scenes and the new scene, which shows him for the duration of a steadily paced eight-minute walk that takes him across a bridge to his appointment. This extended tracking shot is a kind of choreography of the imaginary, a journey within the viewer's experience of Wenders's movie, forefronting our unconscious, subjective assumptions about the time and events in between the cut. Yet Huyghe fills in this cut to add more questions, not to add meaning. Are we witnessing Ganz the actor or the character he played? Who controls what lies between cuts: the director alluding or the viewer inferring? Is "nonaction" in fact the most pregnant part of the drama?

In his work, Huyghe continually seeks to recuperate such in-between spaces and to allow each individual's own voice to determine the duration, timbre, and shape of dramas. *Blanche-Neige Lucie* (1997) opens with a wide shot of a studio and lights being raised. There is no sound, but we read an introductory subtitle, "My encounter with Snow White first began," as the lights illuminate the studio. Instead of introducing us to an unfolding drama of action and dialogue, the film cuts to a shot of Lucie Dolene, an elderly snow-haired woman who looks sweetly at the camera without speaking. While the camera holds on her as she smiles mutely, the subtitles in French relate Lucie's story of how she was chosen to dub the 1962 French version of *Snow White and the Seven Dwarfs* (1937). Thirty years after her original performance, Lucie discovers that Disney has been using her voice recording for other purposes, without authorization. She feels that she gave herself, her voice, completely over to the character, to Snow White—"Absolutely, yes!"—and feels ambivalent about this voice when she learns that it is not only embodied in the animated sketches but has also been leading a separated, parallel existence. She lobbies to reclaim the rights of her disembodied voice and, by doing so, regains her proper voice, one of protest and an assertion of self-ownership. Yet, in the end, who owns whom? Where does true ownership of this Blanche-Neige/Lucie voice lie: within a corporation, a fictional character, an actor, the popular audience, a sound track, a person's self, a larynx?

The voice in *One Million Kingdoms* (2001) is a similarly problematizing one; here it resists attribution to a single individual, character, or even narrative function. This is the latest in a series of animated films by Huyghe in which a brooding young girl named AnnLee—an *anime* character created by a Japanese design firm and "sold" to the artist—is placed within various dramas. In another of these films, *Two Minutes Out of Time* (2000), AnnLee—a vacant figure for hire—says of herself, "While waiting to be dropped into a story, she has been diverted from a fictional existence and has become . . . a deviant sign. Renegade existences of signifiers; a sign without a referent."[2] In *One Million Kingdoms* she is dropped into a terrain that rises and falls in tandem with the rise and fall of the narrator's voice, an at times labored voice meant to simulate the transmission of an astronaut, recalling that of Neil Armstrong's voice during the first manned landing on the moon. The story of that moon landing in 1969 and of Jules Verne's 1864 novel *Journey to the Center of the Earth* have been conflated here in a conspiracy theory of the faked and the fantastic. The astronaut's first

bing, 1996. Color video, 120 minutes. Edition of 3, 1 A.P.

The Third Memory, 1999. Color video, double projection, 9 minutes, 46 seconds. Edition of 4, 1 A.P.

ose, 1998. Color video, triple projection, 13 minutes. Edition of 4, 1 A.P.

nche-Neige Lucie, 1997. S-16/35 mm color film transferred ideo, 3 minutes, 29 seconds. Edition of 3, 1 A.P.

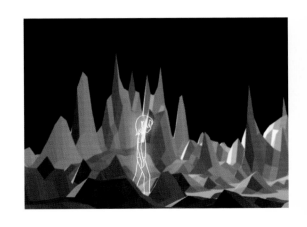

One Million Kingdoms, 2001. Color video, 6 minutes. Edition of 6, 2 A.P.

words, "It's a lie," prompt AnnLee to take her first steps through a constantly fluctuating landscape, whose topography, like a graph of sound waves, is determined by utterance. Yet the voice that prompted AnnLee's actions subsequently seems to emanate from her, as her mouth moves in time, though slightly out of sync, with the voice. This embodied/disembodied voice speaks a language that moves in and out of the fictional and factual, using eerily similar, though distinct, genres: Verne's "novel" with what some call prescient speculations of technology and exploration and Armstrong and Buzz Aldrin's "transmissions," the veracity of which conspiracy theorists call into question. AnnLee, with her fragility as an outlined, semitransparent figure, and the astronaut, with his halting, labored voice, suggest permeable and unstable texts unloosed in space. Moreover, they point to the ever-shifting terrain—in which the lived, the mediated, and the imaginary combine and recombine—of our postmodern condition.

Other potentially loosened signifiers are found in *Atari Light* and *Les Grands Ensembles* (1994–2001), which were installed in rooms adjacent to *One Million Kingdoms* at the Venice *Biennale* in 2001. Overhead lighting panels flicker on and off at seemingly at random, until the viewer realizes that *Atari Light* is an interactive game—Pong—being played out on the ceiling. Is Pong, whose earliest prototype was devised by one of the nuclear scientists involved in the Manhattan Project, meant to have an underlyingly sinister tone in this installation, or is a game just a game? Illuminated grids are also elements of *Les Grands Ensembles*, a projection showing the facades of two multistoried housing complexes. The patterns of lights in the windows suggest unseen inhabitants who brighten or darken rooms, embedding a mysterious code within the most mundane action. As with the electronic tones played by Francois Truffaut's character in *Close Encounters of the Third Kind* (Steven Spielberg, 1977), Huyghe's video reveals a world of correspondences, waiting to be deciphered, reconfigured, and played.

1 Pierre Huyghe, "Freed Time Scenarios," interview by Françoise Chaloin, in *Cinéma Cinéma: Contemporary Art and the Cinematic Experience*, exh. cat. (Eindhoven: Stedelijk Van Abbemuseum, 1999), p. 89.
2 Quoted in Michael Rush, "Pierre Huyghe at Marian Goodman," *Art in America* 89. no. 6 (June 2001), p. 122.

Pierre Huyghe

1962 - Born in Paris
Lives and works in Paris

Selected One-Person Exhibitions

2001 - New York, Marian Goodman
Gallery, *Even More Real Than
You*, Jan. 9–Feb. 10.
- Geneva, Musée d'Art Moderne
et Contemporain, *Vivement 2002
4ème épisode: Pierre Huyghe,
Two Minutes out of Time*,
Feb. 21–Apr. 29.
- Eindhoven, Stedelijk van
Abbemuseum, *Pierre Huyghe:
Interludes*, Feb. 24–May 6.
Catalogue.
- Venice, French Pavilion,
Le Chateau de Turing,
49th Venice *Biennale*,
June 10–Nov. 4.

2000 - Chicago, Museum of Contempo-
rary Art, *Pierre Huyghe: Blanche
Neige Lucie*, March 18–June 25.
- Chicago, The Renaissance
Society, University of Chicago,
Pierre Huyghe: The Third Memory,
Apr. 9–30. Catalogue. Traveled to
Paris, Centre Georges Pompidou,
June 9–Oct. 6; Montreal, Musée
d'Art Contemporain de Montréal,
Oct. 12, 2000–Jan. 7, 2001.
- Paris, Marian Goodman Gallery,
*No Ghost just a Shell: Deux
minutes en dehors du temp*,
May 30–June 25.
- Berlin, Galerie Schipper und
Krome, *No Ghost just a Shell: Two
Minutes out of Time*, Sept. 2–16.

1999 - Aarhus, Denmark, Aarhus Kunst-
museum, *L'Ellipse*, Mar. 16–
Apr. 5. Traveled to Stockholm,
Index, the Swedish Contemporary
Art Foundation, Sept. 4–Oct. 3.
- Vienna, Wiener Secession,
Pierre Huyghe, Apr. 28–June 13.
Catalogue *Pierre Huyghe:
The Trial*. Traveled to Munich,
Kunstverein München, as
*Pierre Huyghe: Some Negotia-
tions*, Oct. 16–Nov. 21; Zurich,
Kunsthalle Zürich, Jan. 15–
Mar. 12, 2000.
- Santa Monica, Santa Monica
Museum of Art, *Côté ouest*,
Sept. 18–Nov. 27. Catalogue.
- Porto, Portugal, Museu de
Serralves, *Pierre Huyghe: L'Ellipse*,
Nov. 19, 1999–Jan. 23, 2000.
Catalogue.

1997 - Dijon, Le Consortium Centre d'Art
Contemporain, *Story Teller*,
Apr. 11–June 14.
- Dijon, Le Consortium Centre d'Art
Contemporain, *Mobile TV*,
Oct. 23–Nov. 9.

1996 - Geneva, Forde Espace d'Art Contemporain, *Daily*, Sept. 5–Oct. 13.

1995 - Montpellier, Fonds Régional d'Art
Contemporain Languedoc
Roussillon, *L'usage de l'interprète*,
March 24–May 6.

Selected Group Exhibitions

2002 - Zurich, Kunsthalle Zürich, *Anna
Lee*, Aug. 24–Oct. 20. Catalogue.

2001 - Rotterdam, Museum Boijmans
van Beuningen, *30th Rotterdam
International Film Festival*,
Jan. 24–Feb. 4.
- Yokohama, First Yokohama
Triennial, Sept. 2–Nov. 11.
Catalogue.
- Ann Arbor, Mich., Jean Paul
Slusser Gallery, University of
Michigan School of Art (organized
by Independent Curators Interna-
tional), *Everything Can Be
Different*, Sept. 11–Nov. 4.
Traveling through Dec. 2003.
- Istanbul, Seventh Istanbul
Biennial, Sept. 22–Nov. 17.
Catalogue.
- Turin, Castello di Rivoli, *Form
Follows Fiction*, Oct. 17, 2001–
Jan. 27, 2002. Catalogue.
- London, Institute of Contemporary
Arts, the Mall, *In Many Ways the
Exhibition Already Happened*,
Dec. 1, 2001–Jan. 20, 2002.

2000 - Minneapolis, Walker Art Center,
Let's Entertain, Feb. 12–Apr. 30.
Catalogue. Traveled to Paris,
Centre Georges Pompidou as
Au delà du spectacle, Nov. 22,
2000–Jan. 8, 2001; Wolfsburg,
Germany, Kunstmuseum
Wolfsburg, March 17–July 15,
2001.
- Paris, Musée d'Art Moderne de la
Ville de Paris, *Voilà: Le monde
dans la tête*, June 15–Oct. 29.
Catalogue.
- Hamburg, Hamburger Kunst-
verein, *Philippe Parreno,
Dominique Gonzalez-Foerster,
Pierre Huyghe*, Oct. 7–Nov. 12.
- Glasgow, Tramway, *Vivre sa vie:
Pierre Huyghe and Philippe
Parreno*, Nov. 17–Dec. 18.
Catalogue.
- San Francisco, San Francisco Art
Institute, Pierre Huyghe and
Philippe Parreno, *Anna Sanders.
The Story of a Feeling Scene 3*,
Dec. 7, 2000–Jan. 20, 2001.

1999 - Eindhoven, Stedelijk van Abbe-
museum, *Cinéma, cinéma:
Contemporary Art and the
Cinematic Experience*, Feb. 13–
May 24. Catalogue.

- Venice, 48th Venice *Biennale*,
June 13–Nov. 7. Catalogue.
- Oxford, Museum of Modern Art,
*Notorious: Alfred Hitchcock and
Contemporary Art*, July 11–
Oct. 3. Catalogue. Traveled to
Sydney, Museum of Contempo-
rary Art, Dec. 19, 1999–Apr. 25,
2000; Hamilton, Art Gallery of
Hamilton, May 20–July 16, 2000;
Odense, Denmark, Kunsthallen
Brandts Klaedefabrik, Aug. 25–
Nov. 12, 2000; Tokyo, Tokyo
Opera City Art Gallery, Apr. 4–
June 17, 2001; Hiroshima,
Museum of Contemporary Art,
July 29–Sept. 2, 2001; Lleida,
Spain, Centro Cultural de la
Fundació La Caixa, Sept. 27–
Nov. 11, 2001; Hasselt, Belgium,
Provinciaal Centrum voor
Beeldende Kunsten, Dec. 8,
2001–Jan. 20, 2002.
- Istanbul, Sixth Istanbul *Biennial*,
Sept. 17–Oct. 30. Catalogue.
- Liverpool, *Liverpool Biennial of
Contemporary Art: Liverpool
Billboard Project*, Sept. 24–Nov. 7,
1999. Catalogue.
- Washington, D.C., Hirshhorn
Museum and Sculpture Garden,
*Regarding Beauty: A View of the
Late Twentieth Century*, Oct. 7,
1999–Jan. 17, 2000. Catalogue.
Traveled to Munich, Haus der
Kunst, Feb. 12–May 21, 2000.
- Pittsburgh, Carnegie Museum of
Art, *Carnegie International*,
Nov. 6, 1999–March 26, 2000.
Catalogue.

1998 - Rotterdam, Witte de With/Center
for Contemporary Art, *Voices*,
June 13–Aug. 23. Catalogue.
Traveled to Barcelona, Fundació
Joan Miró, Sept. 17–Nov. 1;
Tourcoing, France, Le Fresnoy
Studio National des Arts
Contemporains, Feb. 20–
Apr. 4, 1999.
- Luxembourg, Casino
Luxembourg, *Manifesta 2*,
June 28–Oct. 11. Catalogue.
- Sydney, *11th Biennial of Sydney*,
Sept. 15–Nov. 8. Catalogue.
- New York, Guggenheim Museum
SoHo, *Premises: Invested Spaces
in Visual Arts, Architecture and
Design from France, 1958–1998*,
Oct. 15, 1998–Jan. 11, 1999.
Catalogue.
- Paris, Musée d'Art Moderne de
la Ville de Paris, *Dominique
Gonzalez-Foerster, Pierre
Huyghe, Philippe Parreno*,
Oct. 30, 1998–Jan. 10, 1999.
Catalogue.

1997 - Paris, Fondation Cartier,
Coïncidences, Apr. 4–May 18.
Catalogue.

- Venice, 47th Venice *Biennale*,
June 15–Nov. 9. Catalogue.
- Johannesburg, Second
Johannesburg *Biennial*, Oct. 10–
Dec. 18. Catalogue.

1995 - Amsterdam, De Appel Founda-
tion, *Shift*, Apr. 24–May 22.
Catalogue.
- Lyons, *3ème Biennale d'Art
Contemporain de Lyon*, Dec. 20,
1995–Feb. 18, 1996. Catalogue.

Pierre Huyghe

Top left: Original celluloid from *Snow White and the Seven Dwarfs*, 1937.
Other images: Four stills from *Blanche-Neige Lucie*, 1997. S-16/35mm color film transferred to video.

Top (left to right): *The Third Memory*. Production view; clipping from the *Daily News*, August 23, 1972;
detail from *Life* magazine, September 22, 1972.
Middle and bottom: *The Third Memory*, 1999. Color video, double projection.

Top left: *No Ghost Just A Shell* (collaboration with Philippe Parreno), 2000. Silkscreened poster by M/M Paris.
Top right: *Two Minutes Out of Time*, 2000. Color video.
Center right, and opposite page, top and bottom: installation views, Stedelijk Van Abbemuseum, 2001.
Bottom left and right: *One Million Kingdoms*, 2001. Color video.

Les Grands Ensembles, 1994–2001. Vistavision transferred to digital hard disc.
Music by Pan Sonic and Cedric Pigot (random program).

Four exhibition views of *Le Chateau de Turing,* the French Pavilion, 49th Venice *Biennale*, 2001.
Top left: Lighting prototype (collaboration with Philippe Parreno and M/M Paris), 2001.
Top right: *One Million Kingdoms*, 2001 (reflected); and *Atari Light*, 1999. Computer game program, interface,
joysticks, and mixed media.
Bottom left: *Les Grands Ensembles*, 1994–2001.
Bottom right: *Atari Light*, 1999.

Sculpture Degree Zero: Koo Jeong-a

Francesco Bonami

As a thing the way is
Shadowy, indistinct.
Indistinct and shadowy,
Yet within it is an image;
Shadowy and indistinct,
Yet within it is a substance.
Dim and dark,
Yet within it is an essence.
This essence is quite genuine
And within it is something that can be tested.
—Lao Tzu, *Tao Te Ching*

The *Ecstasy of Saint Teresa* by Gianlorenzo Bernini in the Cornaro chapel of the church of Santa Maria della Vittoria in Rome, 1647–52. *Oslo* by Koo Jeong-a in a darkened room somewhere in the world, 1998. The former is a masterpiece of Baroque sculpture, an extremely elaborate marble of the saint having a vision of an angel. Bernini lit the work from a hidden window in the ceiling of the church, suspending the sculpture in a sublime light as if to dissolve the weight of the marble. The latter is a small landscape of crushed aspirin placed on a small wooden base in a corner of a large, dark room. Koo Jeong-a suffused the work with a blue light hidden in the ceiling, illumination that has the temperature of the dawn light in a northern country.

The powder of crushed aspirin produced by Koo Jeong-a in making this diminutive landscape was probably less than the marble powder produced by Bernini in sculpting a finger of Saint Teresa. Koo Jeong-a treated the aspirin like small pieces of marble, but instead of searching for a form within a huge block of stone in the manner of the Baroque sculptor, she extracted the spirit of the matter—its evocative power—to discover the ecstasy inherent in everything of the physical world.

The Baroque and the Tao: The power of movement and emotional intensity and the power of inaction and essence.

A place of the mind and a place of the spirit. *Saint Teresa* and *Oslo*. Both are visions. One drags the viewer into the sensuality of religious experience, the other pushes the viewer toward the experience of enlightenment. These two sculptors, so different from one another, achieve the same goal despite the distance between their respective philosophies and worlds, the West and the East. Both sculptures transport the viewer into an awakened state of consciousness, into a particular flow that erases time, history, and geography.

Herein lies the similarity as well as the distinction between these artists. Bernini reflected a new state of mind, that of the Baroque, the first movement in the history of art after Copernicus's discoveries and the realization that human beings were not the center of the universe, but mere particles in a suddenly borderless cosmos. Koo Jeong-a similarly faces a world aware that it is no longer a closed system but a system of endless possibilities, with endless combinations of rules expanding to create an increasingly complex geography. Within these newly shifted worlds, both artists have created work that plumbs to the core of their beliefs. Bernini was committed to the authority of the Roman Catholic Church and its attempt to celebrate its world centrality despite its displacement from the center of the universe. Koo Jeong-a searches on the path of representation for her own flow; she is committed to the authority of the inner religiosity of the self in a world where newly discovered galaxies and subatomic matter have extended the perceptible universe.

Although Koo Jeong-a does not declare a philosophical or religious belief, it is apparent that her roots stem from a Taoist vision of life, a state of mind that verges on anonymity, into *wu wei* (without action) and *wu ming* (without name), concepts central to Taoist theory. She understands all too well that geographical limitations and cultural specificity are now impossible. She recognizes that "west" and "east" are no more than moving targets: Paris is west of Seoul, but Seoul is west of Los Angeles.

Her artistic genealogy can be traced through the work of Michael Asher, Samuel Beckett, James Lee Byars, John Cage, Marisa Merz, Cecilia Vicuna, and Walt Whitman, who are revealed in her work not as quotations but as an attitude toward reality and space, an attitude that wants to reclaim marginal and peripheral meanings, or hidden or overlooked corners, places where she chooses to connect her ideas and interventions. Is Koo Jeong-a a forerunner of a new generation of artists reflecting upon the legacy of Conceptual art and its capacity to be part of the contemporary discourse? Hardly so. She is an artist adopting a private and intimate strategy rather than a conceptual strategy. She looks to her own identity as the threshold through which a space can be conceived and presented to the outside world. Koo Jeong-a's idea of a work of art, detached from conventionality, does not belong to the space that we are used to thinking about when discussing contemporary art production. Instead, the process of making the work overlaps with the work itself, rendering the product and the energy required to produce it indistinguishable elements.

As Joseph Conrad wrote, "The artist appeals to that part of our being . . . which is a gift and not an acquisition—and therefore, more permanently enduring."[1] Instead of analyzing the context in order to subvert it, as a Conceptual artist might do, Koo Jeong-a organizes her work as a ceremony within the space she is offered. This ceremony leads toward a gift, which is both the work itself and our reaction to it. Invited to participate in a group exhibition, *Unfinished History*, at the Walker Art Center in Minneapolis in 1998, Koo Jeong-a carved out a corner in a gallery to create a shelter in which she hid for most of the installation. Once the shelter was removed, the space looked as empty as before, yet in the lower corner she had filled the gap between the floor and wall with papier-mâché. With precise lighting, an irrelevant space was transformed into a corner of a metaphysical landscape by Giorgio de Chirico, casting a shadow upon the emptiness of the gallery space. The title of the work, no less mysterious than its genesis, was *Humpty Dumpty*. The awkward simplicity and poverty of the work succeeded in retaining an alchemic purity, like the gestures and naïveté of a young monk.

Born in Korea in 1967, Koo Jeong-a has lived in Paris for over a decade. Rather than hybridize her original creative language with her new environment to become part of a community of token foreign artists, she has maintained her distance. Yet, her work has joined two ways of thinking, two ways of conceiving the artistic endeavor—her work is a split screen. On one side is *Saint Teresa*, on the other is *Oslo*. They touch each other, but they do not interfere. Koo Jeong-a's work interacts with the space where she creates it without becoming part of it, like a micromirage, never completely assuming a physical presence. It is as if Paris had become a neighborhood of Seoul, or Seoul a neighborhood of Paris. The two spaces dwell one inside the other, yet are autonomous. Her interventions are visions ready to disappear as suddenly as they appear. Much of her work has the structure of dreams, where elements of daily life are present yet inconsistent. While what we see comes from familiar objects, their transformation makes it difficult to grasp their original forms. *Floating House* (1996), for example, made of sugar cubes and cardboard, is reminiscent of Marcel Duchamp's *Why Not Sneeze Rrose Sélavy?* (1921), a small white birdcage filled with marble cubes that look like sugar. Although we cannot say if Koo Jeong-a consciously quoted Duchamp, we feel that perhaps she could have dreamed her work after seeing his in a textbook or catalogue.

South (2000) is an overheated room with red earth assembled on a table, like cookie dough. When seen from above, the mounds of earth resemble a North African town. This work allows us to understand how the artist's mind and body float between the realms of reality and the subconscious, shifting like the cursor on a computer screen. Various layers of perception produce the meaning of the work: the heat of

Gianlorenzo Bernini, *Ecstasy of Saint Teresa*, 1647–52.
Marble. Santa Maria della Vittoria, Rome.

Oslo, 1998. Aspirin, spotlight, and wood, dimensions variable.

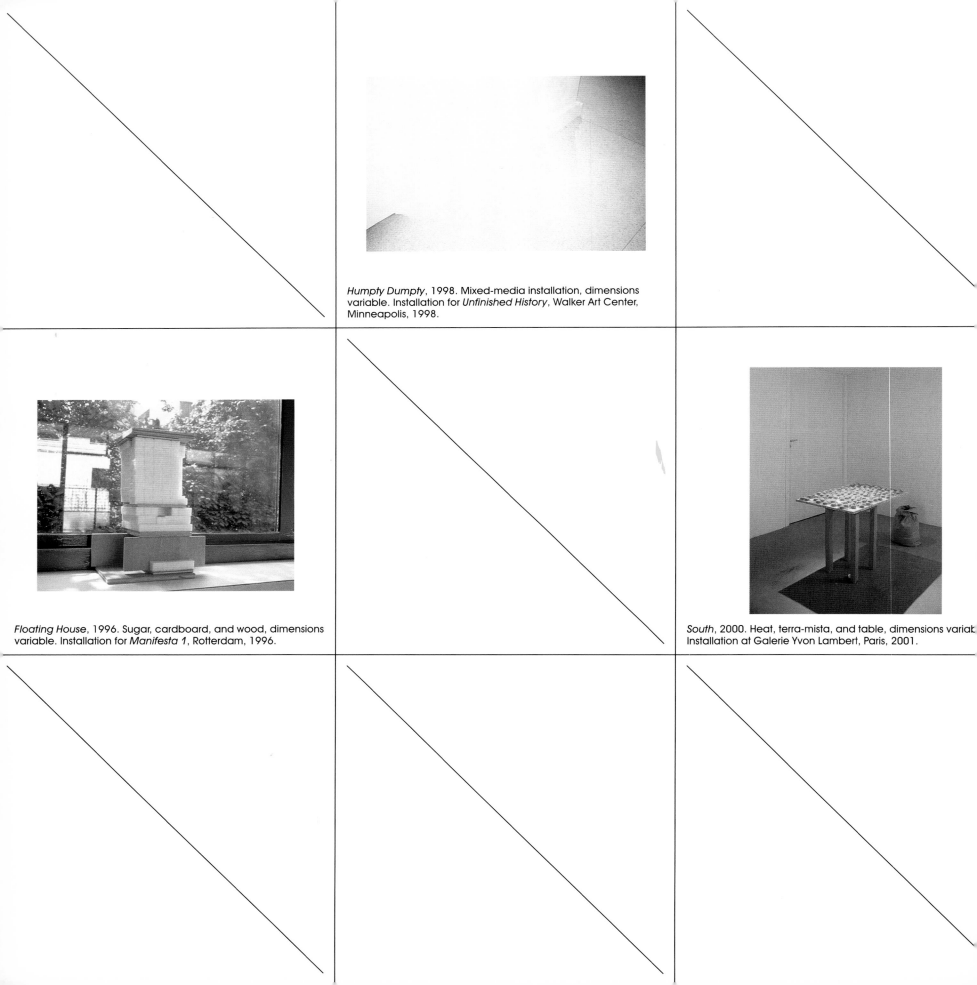

Humpty Dumpty, 1998. Mixed-media installation, dimensions variable. Installation for *Unfinished History*, Walker Art Center, Minneapolis, 1998.

Floating House, 1996. Sugar, cardboard, and wood, dimensions variable. Installation for *Manifesta 1*, Rotterdam, 1996.

South, 2000. Heat, terra-mista, and table, dimensions variab[le]. Installation at Galerie Yvon Lambert, Paris, 2001.

the room, the dusty red color of the clay, the modular shape of the huts. They are like the elements of a memory, meaningless if separate, profound and complete if together or like the famous madeleine of Proust, with its simple flavor that recalls an endless chain of memories.

Definitions are doomed to interpretation and change. Art itself is a shifting idea subjected to varying combinations of private, aesthetic, formal, and conceptual anticipations, convictions, and expectations. Koo Jeong-a works with all of these. Her language, Korean, has been constructed from a system of signs derived from the I Ching. The symbols of the language, unlike those of other Asian languages like Chinese or Japanese, are phonetic, not visual; the symbol is not the visual representation of its meaning. In a way, something similar happens in Koo Jeong-a's work. What we see sometimes is not what is there. Like the I Ching, the artist presents us with combinations of possible meanings, dreams, ideas, and moods to be interpreted or to be accepted simply for their shape, sound, and temperature.

Nothing really exists for Koo Jeong-a because that which has existence also suffers from the limitations of the specific. The crushed aspirin in *Oslo* exists only until the wind blows, until the sun is high, and we awake from our dreams. *Oslo* is the sublime dream of Saint Teresa while the angel pierces her soul with an arrow. Koo Jeong-a's art is a gentle shock to the sensibilities of Western culture, into visions, dreams, memory loss, and the desire to be elsewhere without leaving home. The path of true art is not its goal.

Each of Koo Jeong-a's works, with their presence and absence, negotiates, echoes, and expands Duchamp's question of how to make art without making a work of art. Koo Jeong-a asks how to create something while knowing that it has always been.

1 Joseph Conrad, *The Nigger of the Narcissus* (New York: Doubleday, 1926), p. xii.

Koo Jeong-a

1967 - Born in Seoul
Lives and works in Paris

Selected One-Person Exhibitions

2002 - Dublin, Douglas Hyde Gallery,
The Land of Ouss, Apr. 11–June 1.
Catalogue.

2001 - Kyoto, Shigemori Residence,
Shima/Islands: To Fall to Dive,
Feb. 2–28. Catalogue
forthcoming.
- Paris, Galerie Yvon Lambert,
Koo Jeong-a, May 19–June 30.
Catalogue.

1999 - Paris, Côté Rue; Galerie
Yvon Lambert, *Koo Jeong-a*,
Apr. 29–May 25.

1998 - Stockholm, Moderna Museet,
Moderna Museet Projekt: ∞/24,
May 2–25. Catalogue.

1997 - Paris, 28 rue Rousselet (organized
by L'Association Mobile 2000),
Too://www.so.up/there, Feb. 8, 9,
10, 15, 16, 17, 22, 23, and 24.
Catalogue.
- Paris, Musée d'Art Moderne de
la Ville de Paris, *Aqueduc*,
Apr. 25–June 22. Catalogue.
- Utrecht, Casco Space, *In Out Up
Down*, June 1–29.

1996 - Paris, 16 rue Etienne Marcel,
Armoire du pull-over, May 21–23.

1995 - Paris, Galerie Anne de Villepoix,
Je marche à pied, Mar. 7.

1994 - Paris, Musée d'Art Moderne de la
Ville de Paris, *Migrateurs*, May.
Catalogue.

Selected Group Exhibitions

2002 - Kwangju, Fourth Kwangju
Biennial, Mar. 29–June 29.
Catalogue.
- Seoul, Artsonje Center, *Less
Ordinary*, Apr. 27–June 23.
Catalogue. Scheduled to travel
to Kyongju, Artsonje Museum,
Sept. 14–Dec. 8.

2001 - Venice, 49th Venice *Biennale*
(*En el cielo*), June 13–18.
- Yokohama, First Yokohama
Triennial, Sept. 2–Nov. 11.
Catalogue.
- Ann Arbor, Mich., Jean Paul
Slusser Gallery, University of
Michigan School of Art (organized
by Independent Curators Interna-
tional), *Everything Can Be
Different*, Sept. 11–Nov. 4.

Catalogue. Scheduled to travel
through December 2003.

2000 - Stockholm, International Artists
Studio Program, *Syndrome 1*,
Mar. 31–Apr. 29.
- Aachen, Ludwig Forum for Inter-
national Art; Maastricht,
Bonnefantenmuseum; Heerlen,
Stadsgalerij; Liege, Musée d'Art
Moderne et d'Art Contemporain,
Continental Shift, May 21–
Sept. 10. Catalogue.
- Rome, Villa Medicis, *La ville,
le jardin, la mémoire 1998–2000*,
June 22–Sept. 24. Catalogue.
- Ljubljana, *Manifesta 3*,
June 23–Sept. 24. Catalogue.
- Avignon, Musée d'Art Contempo-
rain, *Rendez-vous: Collection
Lambert*, June 28–Aug. 30.
- Boston, Institute of Contemporary
Art, *From a Distance:
Approaching Landscape*,
July 18–Oct. 8. Catalogue.
- Tokyo, Art Front Gallery, *First
Echigo-Tsumari Art Triennial*,
July 20–Oct. 9. Catalogue.
- Baltimore, Contemporary
Museum, *Snapshot: An Exhibition
of 1,000 Artists*, Nov. 2, 2000–
Feb. 4, 2001. Catalogue.
- Edinburgh, Institut Français
d'Ecosse, *Vivre sa vie*, Nov. 20,
2000–Jan. 31, 2001. Catalogue.
- Bordeaux, CAPC Musée d'Art
Contemporain, *Villes Intimes*,
Nov. 25, 2000–Apr. 1 2001.
- Florence, Biagiotti Progetto Arte,
*Finale di partita, Endgame fin de
partie*, Dec. 16, 2000–Jan. 20,
2001. Catalogue.
- Luxembourg, Musée d'Histoire
de la Ville de Luxembourg,
Ma sorcière bien aimée, Dec. 21,
2000–Feb. 11, 2001.

1999 - New York, PS 1 Contemporary Art
Center, *Generation Z*,
Apr. 18–June 6. Catalogue.
- Antwerp, Provinciaal Museum
voor Fotografie, *Laboratorium*,
June 27–Oct. 3. Catalogue.
- Paris, Musée d'Art Moderne de
la Ville de Paris, *L'autre sommeil*,
Nov. 17, 1999–Jan. 23, 2000.
Catalogue.
- Nantes, France, Fonds Régional
d'Art Contemporain des Pays de
la Loire, *Singulier-Pluriel*, Nov. 23–
Dec. 12.
- Paris, Ecole Nationale Supérieure
des Beaux-Arts, *Nous nous
sommes tant aimés*, Dec. 14,
1999–Feb. 13, 2000. Catalogue.

1998 - Saint-Cloud, France, *Le printemps
de cahors: La sphère de l'intime*,
May 29–June 19. Catalogue.

- Dijon, Fonds Régional d'Art
Contemporain Bourgogne, *Dust
Memories*, June 13–Sept. 5.
- Minneapolis, Walker Art Center,
Unfinished History, Oct. 18,
1998–Jan. 10, 1999. Catalogue.
- Bilbao, Sala Rekalde, *¡Silencio!*,
Dec. 1, 1998–Jan. 10, 1999.
- Luxembourg, Casino
Luxembourg, *Gare de l'est*,
Dec. 12, 1998–Feb. 21, 1999.

1997 - Palo Alto, Calif., Palo Alto Cultural
Center (organized by Indepen-
dent Curators International), *Do It*,
June 15–July 27. Catalogue.
Traveled to multiple venues
through Dec. 2001.
- Kwangju, Second Kwangju
Biennial, Sept. 1–Nov. 27.
Catalogue.
- Paris, Ecole Nationale Supérieure
des Beaux-Arts, *Transit*, Sept. 16–
Nov. 2. Catalogue.
- Vienna, Wiener Secession, *Cities
on the Move*, Nov. 26, 1997–
Jan. 18, 1998. Catalogue.
Traveled to Bordeaux, CAPC
Musée d'Art Contemporain,
June 4–Aug. 30, 1998; New York,
PS 1 Contemporary Art Center,
Oct. 18 1998–Jan. 3, 1999;
Humlebaek, Denmark, Louisiana
Museum of Modern Art, Jan. 29–
Apr. 21, 1999; London, Hayward
Gallery, May 13–June 27, 1999;
Bangkok, (multiple venues),
Oct. 9–30; Helsinki, Kiasma
Museum of Contemporary Art,
Nov. 11, 1999–Jan. 9, 2000.

1996 - Rotterdam, *Manifesta 1*,
June 9–Aug. 19. Catalogue.
- Paris, Ecole Nationale Supérieure
des Beaux-Arts, *L'art du plastique*,
Sept. 20–Nov. 10.

1995 - Paris, Galerie Anne de Villepoix;
Société Jet Lag K, *Tu parles/
J'écoute*, June 3–July 23.
Catalogue. Traveled to Taipei,
Taipei Fine Arts Museum,
Jan. 24–Mar. 29, 1998;
Marne-la-Valée, Le Centre d'Art
Contemporain de la Ferme
du Buisson, Nov. 17, 1998–
Jan. 31, 1999.
- Venice, 47th Venice *Biennale*,
June 11–Oct. 15. Catalogue.

Koo Jeong-a

Anri Sala: Reverse of the Real

Jörg Heiser

In his book *Pandora's Hope*, Bruno Latour, doyen of science studies, recounts an Indian story.[1] Jagannath, a Brahman, is determined to bring about a revelation for the pariahs gathered in the courtyard of his family's estate. He grabs the sacred stone that indicates his caste and crosses the forbidden, in-between zone toward the slaves in order to make them touch and thus desecrate the stone. They shrink back, faces torn with fear, and in Jagannath's eyes become revolting, creeping creatures. In a wrathful voice he orders, "Touch it now!" And they mechanically do what they are told.

Jagannath's attempt to enlighten—to dismantle the magic justification of subordination, to simply erase inequality by "revealing," self-righteously, that the stone is just a stone—has turned into a blunt accusation of the pariahs' supposed naive belief. But what if, ironically, he alone really believes in the stone's magic? What if the slaves are scared not of the stone but of Jagannath's violent act?

The great problem with a gesture of enlightening revelation—in science, politics, or art—is that it categorically presupposes that there are those who know fact from fabrication, reality from fiction, and those who don't. But what if the fabricated still has factual effects? What if those "who don't know" have a different, not necessarily less valuable, knowledge about these factual effects?

The experience of post-Wall Eastern Europe was one of a rupture of any status quo. For those reaching adulthood after 1989 it was not an option to simply "reveal" to the parent generation that the socialist promise of social justice and equality had become a functionalized fiction in the reality of dictatorship; the parents already knew. Maybe—as in the case of Anri Sala, born in Albania in 1974—this experience sharpened the understanding that in order to come to terms with history you have to grapple with the distinction between fact and fabrication. Sala's works make clear that this grappling is also, if not predominantly, an aesthetic task.

Intervista—quelques mots pour le dire (1997) includes found black-and-white footage of Sala's mother being interviewed in the late 1970s, when she was an official of Albania's communist youth organization. He shows her the interview, which is missing its sound track, and she seems more amused than shocked. A kind of detective story ensues with Sala finally reconstructing her words by having deaf mutes read her lips. Finishing the interview with a coquettish smile, as if proud of having done her homework well, she had said, "Examining the current political situation, not only in certain countries but around the world as well, and by discussing problems, we can appreciate the importance of a people's revolutionary movement." Her son sits beside her, and together, with warm feelings, they look at the footage again, reading the now subtitled words out loud. "I don't believe this! It's absurd," she exclaims. "It's just spouting words."

Most scenes in *Intervista* are openly shown as being staged. For example, when Sala meets his mother in her apartment, the camera is there awaiting his arrival, recording the scene as if for a family soap opera. The staged character has two strong effects. First, it heightens rather than lowers the factual effect of the found footage. Like the play within the play in *Hamlet*, the confrontation of two layers of "mediated" reality triggers a credible discourse about truth: in Shakespeare's *Hamlet*, whether the king killed his brother; in Sala's *Intervista*, what the mother said in the interview. Second, it allows the mother "to play along," to play an active role in the reassessment, rather than being subjected to the "J'accuse!" style of Jagannath.

Nocturnes (1999), as with *Intervista*, contaminates documentation with fiction, matter-of-factness with dreaminess, public with intimate, speech with speechlessness. Sala juxtaposes portraits of two seemingly very different men who, nevertheless, appear to have more and more in common as *Nocturnes* unfolds. A nerdy guy walks his dog at night, carrying a live fish in a plastic bag filled with water. He comes home, where the dimly lit space is filled with aquariums. Sala plays with the visual language of fictional cinema—glistening nighttime streets, elegant camera movements, swoosh sounds accompanying close-ups of swimming fish—but as soon as the protagonist explains why he loves his pets, it becomes clear this is a documentary.

The second protagonist served as a United Nations soldier in Bosnia. We only see his hands. As he explains how he was drilled and told to always keep his gun with him, his hands alternate between forming a heart and a cocky gesture of aiming with back sight and bead. Then, resting four fingers of his right hand in the palm of his left, he says he cannot manage to forget that he killed four people on July 24, 1995. Now the ex-soldier kills time and insomnia with shoot-out games on his PlayStation. Meanwhile, the fish lover explains that the new fish has to remain in the plastic bag for a while; the other fish would kill it unless they first get used to its presence. The fish in the bag is a dreamlike metonymy of both men, who are trapped in little worlds and have lost the ability to adjust, to mingle, to express, to sleep. The fictive and factual amalgam that triggers this insight into the void of masculinity switches among four media realities: documentary; scenic film language; video games; and, on an allegoric level, fish moving in an aquarium as if on a screen.

In subsequent works, Sala has accelerated his technique of dialectic juxtaposition to more abstract levels. The camera in *Byrek* (2000) is transfixed by the hands of a woman making the dough for the eponymous Albanian pastry. The camera angle does not change when she walks out of frame to get an ingredient. Only when the sound of an airplane is heard does the camera move, tilting up from the table to the window in order to find the plane and then tilting back. It is as if the plane is competing with the spiral of dough, linear movement with circular, open world with closed, modernity with tradition, generation with generation. The piece was triggered by a letter Sala received from his grandmother, who lives in Albania, and this letter is printed onto the projection screen. Worried about him not eating enough, she tells him her byrek recipe, thus evoking childhood memories. But because he is in France there is no direct access to her or these memories.

From *Byrek* on, Sala's work has gradually moved from narration toward abstraction, to an extent moving from cinema toward art. Traditionally, the cinema is a place where we expect to be submerged in a scenario, almost forgetting our own physical presence—more so with blockbuster films, less so, but still, with documentary cinema. We get annoyed if a movie, even a difficult art-house film, fails to "draw us in." In contrast, the "white cube" of the gallery allows for a mode of perception that is about a tension between contemplation and confrontation while traversing spaces, the viewer relating his/her bodily position in space to the one of the artwork. Sala's works—with their twisting relations between reverie and reality check, circular and linear models of time—benefit from being shown in the art context with its heightened relational awareness.

Uomo Duomo (2000) is almost a paradigmatic abstraction of the artist's juxtapositions. It consists of a single sixty-second shot of an old man sitting on a church bench, fast asleep. Whether he is homeless or someone just taking a nap is an open question. His head curls on his chest as if he is about to wake up. The promenade of tourists going straight to the altar does not wake him. Their linear movement and his circular doze pass one another, as it were, without touching. *Promises* (2001) packs the two narrative models—linear and circular—into one. Four young men, apparently friends of Sala and of his age and nationality, are asked to deliver an Al Capone quotation in deadpan fashion: "Nobody puts a price on my head and lives." The first three each repeat it twice, altering the emphasis, raising an eyebrow to look cool, trying to suppress a smile. This could go on forever, one protagonist after another. The fourth, however, simply fails to deliver the quote, for minutes and minutes. One moment it

rvista—quelques mots pour le dire, 1997. Color video, 26 minutes. Edition of 6.

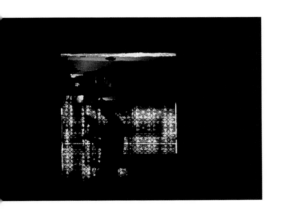

nes, 1999. Color video, 11 minutes, 28 seconds. Edition of 6.

Byrek, 2000. Color video, 21 minutes, 43 seconds. Edition of 6.

Promises, 2001. Color video, 4 minutes, 10 seconds. Edition of 6.

Arena, 2001. Color video, 4 minutes, 38 seconds. Edition of 6.

looks like he is just about to say it, the next like he is permanently paralyzed. "What if I get stuck in the middle? Get blocked?" A voice off camera responds, "Last try and we're gonna watch the movie. OK?" Now it looks as if he is plucking up his courage, conjuring up that one sentence inside him. "Nobody puts a price on my head and lives," he says twice, flawlessly.

The last protagonist's Hamlet-like hesitation breaks the piece's staged character. The cycle of repetition is broken, and time is stretched linearly. The disconnection of speech from protagonist already encountered in *Intervista* is echoed with an ironic twist. This boyish game of posture comes eerily close to the postsocialist reality these young men may live in—an environment, marked by poverty and crime, in which a local Al Capone may be a factual part of the paralyzed sociopolitical climate.

Missing Landscape (2001) has a similar tension between boyish game and abyss but both more literally and more abstractly than in *Promises*. Boys playing soccer in an apparent valley are filmed in a strict symmetric order. Positioned in the middle of the gravel field, the camera is fixed on one and then the other of the wooden goals. Sometimes a goalkeeper vanishes behind an incline before returning with the ball, and as we watch—lulled by the lazy ease of the playing, at times bordering on scrapping—we notice that the same scenes turn up again. Linear time progression is replaced by symmetric repetition. The incline behind the goal is a synecdoche for the entire scene: the ball, the gravel field, the whole valley, maybe the whole of Albania is out of joint, vanished into a loophole of history.

Arena (2001) is Sala's most abstract piece to date; it has no protagonists apart from animals, no story, no speech. The camera tracks slowly left to right, right to left, looking out from a Dan Graham-like pavilion in a run-down park. We see vistas of trees, haystacks, housing blocks, and stray dogs. Strange animal sounds reverberate from the distance. Wild boar? Elephants? Hippopotamuses? The camera pans until a cage covered by rusty fencing comes into sight—this must be a zoo—and moves in closer to reveal the outline of a wild animal. We can only guess what it is before the piece ends. *Arena* and *Missing Landscape* seem to present the neglected place that precedes the very ideas of linear and circular, fact and fiction—the milieu where these concepts themselves arise from furtive insecurity and rough beauty.

1 Bruno Latour, *Die Hoffnung der Pandora. Untersuchungen zur Wirklichkeit der Wissenschaft* (Frankfurt: Suhrkamp, 2000), pp. 330–31. Published in English as *Pandora's Hope: An Essay on the Reality of Science Studies* (Cambridge, Mass.: Harvard University Press, 1999).

Anri Sala

1974 - Born in Tirana, Albania
Lives and works in Paris

Selected One-Person Exhibitions

2002 - Dallas, Dallas Museum of Art,
Concentrations 41: Anri Sala,
Jan. 24–May 20.
- New York, Trans>Area, *Anri Sala,*
Feb. 20–Apr. 6.
- Zurich, Galerie Hauser and Wirth,
Anri Sala: Amplified Absorbers,
Mar. 16–May 11.
- Birmingham, England, Ikon
Gallery, *Anri Sala,* Sept. 25–
Nov. 10.

2001 - London, Delfina Project Space,
Anri Sala: Nocturnes, Apr. 27–
June 3.
- Paris, Galerie Chantal Crousel,
*Anri Sala: It Has Been Raining
Here,* Oct. 6–Nov. 24.
- Berlin, Kunst-Werke, Institut für Zeit-
genössische Kunst und Theorie,
Anri Sala, Nov. 28, 2001–Jan. 13,
2002.

2000 - Munich, Galerie Rüdiger Schöttle,
Intervista, Jan. 26–Mar. 2.
- Cologne, Johnen et Schöttle,
Anri Sala, Sept. 8–Nov. 4.
- Geneva, Musée d'Art Moderne et
Contemporain, *Vivement 2002
3. episode: Anri Sala, Nocturnes,*
Oct. 10, 2000–Jan. 21, 2001.
- Amsterdam, De Appel
Foundation, *Anri Sala,*
Nov. 4, 2000–Jan. 7, 2001.
Catalogue.

Selected Group Exhibitions

2002 - Tourcoing, France, Le Fresnoy
Studio National des Arts Contem-
porains, *C'est pas du cinéma!,*
Jan. 26–Mar. 24.
- São Paulo, *25. Bienal Interna-
cional de São Paulo,* Mar. 23–
June 2. Catalogue.
- Turin, Big, *Big Social Game,*
Apr. 19–May 19.

2001 - Stuttgart, Künstlerhaus,
Passwor(l)ds, Feb. 23–Apr. 29.
- Berlin, Second Berlin *Biennial,*
Apr. 20–June 20. Catalogue.
- New York, PS 1 Contemporary Art
Center, *Uniform: Order and Disor-
der,* May 20–Sept. 3. Catalogue.
- Vienna, Wiener Festwochen,
Künstlerhaus Wien, *Du biest die
Welt,* June 1–24.
- Frankfurt, Frankfurter Kunstverein,
Neue Welt, June 1–Sept. 23.
Catalogue.
- Siena, Italy, Palazzo delle
Papesse, *The Gift: Generous
Offerings, Threatening Hospitality,*

June 3–Sept. 23. Catalogue.
Scheduled to travel through
spring 2004.
- Venice, 49th Venice *Biennale,*
June 10–Nov. 4. Catalogue.
- Watou, Belgium, Watou
Poëziezomer, July 1–Sept. 10.
Catalogue.
- Berlin, Institut für Auslands-
beziehungen Galerie Berlin,
*Beautiful Strangers: Art from
Albania,* Aug. 17–Oct. 14.
Catalogue. Traveled to Bonn,
Institut für Auslandsbeziehungen
Galerie Bonn, Jan. 23–Mar. 24,
2001.
- Yokohama, First Yokohama
Triennial, Sept. 2–Nov. 11.
Catalogue.
- Belgrade, Museum of Modern
Art, *Conversations,* Sept. 9–
Dec. 10.
- Tirana, Albania, First Tirana
Biennial, Sept. 10–Oct. 15.
Catalogue.
- Berlin, Haus der Kulturen der Welt,
Unpacking Europe, Sept. 14–
Nov. 11. Catalogue. Traveled
to Rotterdam, Boijmans van
Beuningen, Dec. 13, 2001–
Feb. 24, 2002.
- Colchester, England, Firstsite,
Trauma, Sept. 15–Nov. 17.
Traveled to Oxford, Museum
of Modern Art, Jan. 25–Apr. 7,
2002.
- Münster, Westfaltischer
Kunstverein, *Believe,* Sept. 21–
Oct. 28.
- Berlin, Kunst-Werke, Institut für
Zeitgenössische Kunst und
Theorie, *Arrêt sur image,
Zeitgenössische Kunst, aus
Frankreich,* Sept. 29–Nov. 18.
- Graz, Steirischer Herbst, *Abbild:
Portraiture and Depiction,*
Oct. 6–Dec. 16.
- Düsseldorf, Kunstsammlung
im Ständehaus, *Solos for Video,*
Nov. 4–Dec. 15.

2000 - Frankfurt, Frankfurter Kunstverein,
*Man muss ganz schön viel
lernen um hier zu funktionieren,*
Jan. 12–Mar. 12.
- New York, *Fourth Williamsburg
Brooklyn Film Festival,* May 3–9.
- Graz, Rotor Association for
Contemporary Art, *Wie Weg
Disappeared,* May 20–July 1.
Brochure.
- Paris, Musée d'Art Moderne de la
Ville de Paris, *Voilà: Le monde
dans la tête,* June 7–Oct. 29.
Catalogue.
- Rome, Villa Medicis, *La ville,
le jardin, la mémoire 1998–2000,*
June 22–Sept. 24. Catalogue.
- Ljubljana, *Manifesta 3,*
June 23–Sept. 24. Catalogue.
- Seoul, Metropolitan Museum,

*Media City Seoul 2000, City
Vision: Clip City,* Sept. 2–Oct. 31.
Catalogue.
- Florence, Biagiotti Progetto Arte,
*Finale di partita, Endgame fin de
partie,* Dec. 16, 2000–Jan. 20,
2001. Catalogue.

1999 - Venice, 48th Venice *Biennale,*
June 13–Nov. 17. Catalogue.
- Stockholm, Moderna Museet,
*After the Wall: Art and Culture in
Post-Communist Europe,* Oct. 16,
1999–Jan. 16, 2000. Catalogue.
Traveled to Budapest, Ludwig
Museum, June 16–Aug. 27.
- New York, *33rd Annual New York
Exposition of Short Film and
Video,* Dec. 1–5.

Anri Sala

They all lived happily ever after and had lots of children, 2002.

Found family photographs from the 1920s of Albanian emigrants living in the United States. These images were sent back to relatives in Tirana, Albania.

CORBIT
STUDIO

Contributors

Francesco Bonami, a curator and critic, is Manilow Senior Curator of Contemporary Art at the Museum of Contemporary Art, Chicago, and artistic director of the Fondazione Sandretto ReRebaudengo per l'Arte, Turin, and Pitti Immagine Discovery, Florence. He was recently appointed Director of the 50th Venice *Biennale*.

Susan Cross, Assistant Curator at the Solomon R. Guggenheim Museum, organized the exhibition of 2000 Hugo Boss Prize recipient Marjetica Potrč. In 1999, she co-curated *Changing Perceptions: The Panza Collection at the Guggenheim Museum* at the Guggenheim Museum Bilbao and *Venice/Venezia: California Art from the Panza Collection at the Guggenheim Museum* for the Peggy Guggenheim Collection, Venice.

Yuko Hasegawa is Chief Curator of the Twenty-first Century Museum of Contemporary Art, Kanazawa, Japan, which is currently under construction. She recently organized an exhibition of Shirin Neshat's work as part of a series of pre-opening events for the museum. The artistic director of the Seventh International Istanbul *Biennial* (2001), Hasegawa is also on the faculty at Tokyo University of Fine Arts and Music.

Jörg Heiser is an associate editor and frequent contributor to *frieze* magazine. Heiser recently contributed to the monograph *Doug Aitken* (London: Phaidon Press, 2001). He lives and works in Berlin.

Nico Israel is Assistant Professor of English at Hunter College, City University of New York, and is currently on the faculty of the Bard College Center for Curatorial Studies and Art in Contemporary Culture, Annandale-on-Hudson, New York. A frequent contributor to *Artforum*, he is also the author of *Outlandish: Writing Between Exile and Diaspora* (Stanford University Press, 2000).

James Rondeau is Associate Curator of Contemporary Art at the Art Institute of Chicago. In 2001, he served as the co-commissioner for the United States Pavilion at the 49th Venice *Biennale*. At the Art Institute in 2000, Rondeau organized Olafur Eliasson's first one-person exhibition in the United States. His recent publications include articles on artists Ghada Amer, Alighiero e Boetti, and Rineke Dijkstra.

Maria-Christina Villaseñor is Associate Curator of Film and Media Arts at the Solomon R. Guggenheim Museum. She has written on photography, film, and video art for numerous publications, including *Performing Arts Journal* and *The Paris Review*, and co-edited a special issue of *Art Journal* devoted to video art.

COMA interdisciplinary art/design/media studio, based in Brooklyn and Amsterdam, was founded in 1996 by principals Cornelia Blatter and Marcel Hermans. Recent projects include *Nanoarchitecture* (Princeton Architectural Press, 2002); *Fred Tomaselli*, an exhibition catalogue for the Palm Beach Institute of Contemporary Art, Florida; and *Relocated: Twenty Sculptures by Isamu Noguchi from Japan* for the Isamu Noguchi Garden Museum, Queens, New York. In 2001, COMA was an *ID Magazine* Design Review winner.

Captions and photo credits

Blanche-Neige Lucie, 1997. S-16/35mm color film transferred to video, 3 minutes, 29 seconds. Edition of 3, 1 A.P.; p. 73, from left to right: *The Third Memory*, 1999. Production view; clipping from the *Daily News*, August 23, 1972; detail from *Life* magazine, September 22, 1972; middle and bottom: *The Third Memory*, 1999. Color video, double projection, 9 minutes, 46 seconds. Edition of 4, 1 A.P.; p. 74, top left: *No Ghost Just a Shell* (collaboration with Philippe Parreno) 2000. Silkscreened poster by M/M Paris; top right: *Two Minutes Out of Time*, 2000. Color video, 4 minutes. Edition of 4, 2 A.P.; right middle, and p. 75: *Interludes*, exhibition views, Stedelijk Van Abbemuseum, 2001; bottom left and right: *One Million Kingdoms*, 2001. Color video, 6 minutes. Edition of 6, 2 A.P.; p. 76: *Les Grands Emsembles*, 1994–2001. Vistavision transferred to digital hard disc, 7 minutes, 41 seconds (continuous loop). Music by Pan Sonic and Cedric Pigot (random program). Edition of 5, 2 A.P.; p. 77: Four exhibition views of *Le Chateau de Turing*, the French Pavilion, 49th Venice *Biennale*, 2001: top left: Lighting Prototype (collaboration with Philippe Parreno and M/M Paris), 2001; top right: *One Million Kingdoms*, 2001 (reflected); and *Atari Light*, 1999. Computer game program, interface, joysticks, and mixed media. Edition of 2, 1 A.P.; bottom left: *Les Grands Ensembles*, 1994–2001; bottom right: *Atari Light*, 1999.

Koo Jeong-a
pp. 86–87, *Snowy Sunny Day*, 1997. Dust, paper, staples, and mixed media, dimensions variable. Installation at Vienna Secession, 1997; pp. 88–89: *Untitled*, 2000. Paint and light, dimensions variable. Installation at Galerie Yvon Lambert, Paris, 2001; pp. 90–91: *Untitled*, 2001. Shelving, figurines, neon, and paper, dimensions variable. Installation at Galerie Yvon Lambert, Paris, 2001.

Anri Sala
pp. 99–106: *They all lived happily ever after and had lots of children*, 2002. Found photographs on paper, dimensions variable.